THE

SEXLESS

MARRIAGE

SYLVIA BAYATI

KINGDOM KOME PUBLISHING

The Sexless Marriage Published by:

Kingdom Kome Publishing

P.O. Box 720358

Byram, MS 39272

Art & Cover Design: Darryl A. Barnes

ISBN: 978-0-9844242-0-7 (sc)
ISBN: 978-0-9844242-1-4 (ebk)

Printed in the United States by Morris Publishing®
3212 East Highway 30
Kearney, NE 68847
1-800-650-7888

Disclaimer: While these chapters have a point of view concerning marriage, in no case do I describe a marital lifestyle with the intention of endorsing or recommending one particular course of action, since what would work in one marriage would be a failure in another. The publisher and author disclaim liability for any medical advice or relationship advice and their outcomes that may occur as a result of applying the methods suggested in this book. It is recommended that you seek a physician's advice before embarking on any medical program or treatment.

Although this book is not written by a guru, self-proclaimed expert, or medical licensed expert, it is based upon the author's own observation and experience, interviews, and research. All efforts have been made to ensure the accuracy of the information contained in this book as of the date of its publication.

To My Husband

This book would not be complete

Without celebrating my husband **Masoud** of 34 years

Certainly no small feat with the joy, trials, test and tears

Seeing you through God eyes, a heart of gold

That only God has chosen to mold

He assigned you in my care

Only he knows where

We're destined to be.

Love Unconditional!

I LOVE YOU

Dedications

This Book is Dedicated to:

Merieta
Our favorite firstborn daughter…Merieta, who lives life beyond
the norm of our expectations
Maya Angelou says it best "Phenomenal Woman"
With Jesus on your side
Your business, *Girlie Girl Shop*, and other ventures cannot be
denied
Continuously soaring to higher heights
The success of them has already taken flight
Keep on soaring Merieta; do your thang! Love ya bunches.

Milan
Much, much love to our favorite middle daughter Milan
Not small in stature, but standing tall
Continue running life's course well
And watch God do exploits with the sell
Of your business…*Milanique Designs*.

Mitra
Although you are the last of our children
Our love is in abundance for you
You…favorite daughter Mitra are first class
Live your best life with the sass you possess!

Myron
To our only and favorite son…Myron
What more can we say
Always paving the way
And helping us to stay grounded
Renaissance and Trailblazer and Entrepreneur you are

Not allowing your race in this world to be swift
Setting a pace that will endure to the end
Although life brings many a trial
You send everyone a message of hope with that smile!
You all are the reason that I have strived
So you all would not be denied
Hoping to give you exposure to a better way of living and
by example showing you that "yes we can" achieve if we *believe*
With God, nothing is impossible.

Special Dedication to: Our Adorable Grands

Trent who is truly God sent. **Trenton Ray Hannah**
Like manna from heaven, oh so sweet,
A great treat

Damian aka "Dang Dang" was certainly made one of a kind
So expressive and voice so distinct and angelic!
God said, you he made very precious of a gem and a rare find.

Mariah Emijah Griffin…a princess with finesse and mystique
God breathed on you and truly made you beautiful and unique.

Godchild: **Victor Charles Griffin**…Victorious and a champion

in your own right.

Special Dedication

Give it up for my mother, literally who is like none other "**Mary Alice Bolden Barnes Pleasant**" Aka "**Motherdear**". When the storm of life was raging, she held her *peace*. Now, she wears her *piece* (45 caliber lol). She certainly makes it clear that no matter your demise; you truly could hold your head up and the skies are always in reach. I would always hear you say, "I could have done this or I could have done that". Those words would inspire me to write and dedicate this poem to you:

You Could Have

You Could Have aborted us in the womb
Yet you chose to give us room
To live out our best life
You Could Have stepped in pride
And denied us the finer things in life
That you so freely would give and sacrificed
You know: the $2 or $3 dollars we look for in the mail
The Same letters and cards
Each week/month you did not fail to send
The food you would drop off at 5 or 6 in the morning
You say You Could Have finished school
And would have made your mark
*But don't ya know! God gave you the best tool for a great start
Mother wit, a woman's intuition, common sense
Wisdom, knowledge and understanding from above
Let us not forget your unconditional love
He also gave you God the Father, Son & Holy Ghost
Oh…a Born Again Degree, that certainly counts the most!!!
So wear your BA degree well, cause them burning in hell
They be yelling…If only I had that BA degree
I would really be free
So leave the coulda, woulda, shoulda in the past
To us you'll always be first class
Anyhow, only what you do for Christ will last!

Salute to My Father

Lewis Webster Barnes, aka "Mydaddy" as we would say.
As you abide in the heavenly place, I would like to express that
you are missed. I could list the many things that are imprinted in
my remembrance of you. The things that stand out the most, is
when you gave us a host of biblical teachings. I give you honor
and respect.

CONTENTS

Acknowledgements

To the only one who gets all the glory for allowing me to live and tell another side of the story about "The Sexless Marriage". Don't have to sit back and wonder how I made it over, 'cause I know how! Had it not been for *His* Amazing Grace and the Blood of Jesus! Jehovah Jireh! The *Almighty God*! Creator of heaven and earth! Thank you Jesus!!!

To my sisters and brothers, although too numerous to name, yet I must. Because I do not want to hear them fuss that I had neglected and selected some over the rest. So I will recognize each of you by name. I will give you your deserved one minute of fame.

Ouida Faye-would not delay in reminding us of birthdays, events and the family planner. Baby sis, your presence truly is missed when you are not around. In you, sincere love truly is found. Love ya very, very much!

Fran- can always be depended upon for giving us the plan of salvation. I'll always remember that your heart can be tender toward us so that we will wind up in the "masters" hand. Much much love!

Loistean- who was clearly seen as the "Queen". God gave me a sister who was keen and kept it real. You were the one I could physically call and lean on when life issues were too hard to deal with. My therapist lol! Forever grateful and love, love, love!

My big sister "Barbara Jean"- the cream of the crop and I want to stop and give you your long overdue props. Love and Kisses!

Charles- definitely belongs with the stars cause he was on the show "Star Struck"! One-man band and a renaissance man is he! Awesome love for you older brother!

Vic- hardest working brother in the city. Oh so serious and witty. All around entrepreneur, business owner! Love ya much big brother!

Jerry- whom we had to unfortunately bury at a young age. I do recall him being small in stature and a warrior in his own way. I do know I will see him again one day.

Sherman- has a sermon of praise that would shift you in a glorious daze. Love ya much!

Wilford- soared in anything he would put his mind to. Did not matter if he did not have a clue! He would find a way to do it top notch. Always and forever loving you!

Michael- aka "Mike" you would really like. He would keep things orderly and oh so so right. When he enters praise and such a worshiper is he, you are amazed and can't help falling on bended knee. Love always and forever!

Darryl- a barrel of fun and is the youngest of us all. He always would find the time to give us a call. Sending lots of sisterly love your way!

Special Thanks to my Wonderful Sister-in-Laws

Annette Barnes(Darryl), Lakeva Barnes(Wilford), Adrienne Barnes(Sherman), Olivia Barnes(Albert), Helen Johnson, Linda Barnes(Jerry), Gloria Williams(Charles), Lois Johnson(Victor), Felicia Johnson(Bernard)

Super Thanks to Nieces and Nephews

Your future looks bright. Walk in faith, mercy & grace. Shine your light!

Special Kudos

My *bff, Lyvonne Robinson* of San Antonio, Tx…thanks 4 all the love & support & listening ear.

My favorite cousin (*Dorothy Mathews*)…ya know you're loved so so much!

Lora Griffin, bff, who's always been a consolation and a dear!

Sister-in-Christ & *bff "Robin Snell"*…thanks 4 holding me accountable & telling it like it is.

Sister-in-Christ & *bff* *"Loretta Paitts"*…shoot-it-to-ya-straight sister. Soul sister for life & *bff* Deborah Smith from Atlanta. *International Perfecting Outreach Ministries* (Bishop George G.W. Luvene & Fist Lady, Mother Luvertis Luvene…thanks for support and prayers through the years.)

Special Special Kudos

Dr. Hurtestine Wilkerson, Editor in Chief, is a God-sent phenomenal woman. Dr. Janet Vincent kept it oh so real….love you much! Merieta Bayati, Assistant Editor and Social Media. Wanda Ross, *bff*, thanks for all the beauty tips, fun and prayers.

INTRODUCTION

Harold pushed the petal to the metal as he was driving on a two-lane highway and nearly committed suicide. It was because of his ducking and dodging of his wife's irate and combative licks that felt like a ton of bricks. It was becoming an unbearable load for him to deal with. Jennie Sue almost lost her mind because her spouse became unkind with his loud cursing, pushing and shoving, or his constantly hitting, which always was unbefitting. Lakesha almost bit her nail to a pus after discovering love letters in the mail written to her spouse; she confronted him and it led to a huge fuss. Often these problems that couples have to deal with in their relationships can drive them nuts, leave them to rust, make them lose the sizzle and bring out the chizzle or fizzle.

The Sexless Marriage is an added problem that at least *one* in a marriage really could do without. Nevertheless, this is an issue that couples face across America in the twenty-first century. Sexless Marriages is a real issue that has been kept in the closet for years. This is an issue of supreme importance that needs to be addressed in this modern society. The sexless marriage is part of a growing cultural phenomenon that seems to be startling, sad, frustrating, incomprehensible and far-fetched.

~ 1 ~

INTRODUCTION

Didn't you expect sex to be happening in every *legally* married couple's bedroom? Couples that have a license to operate their sex drives and slide down Ecstasy Island are struggling with the brakes. Whereas, on the other hand, the single folks who *don't have license* are ready to have sex; so their brakes are screeching the pavements. Could you and your spouse become a part of this sexless lifestyle? Perhaps some of you grew up hearing and seeing some of your elderly grandparents sleeping in separate beds or bedrooms. Hmn! The sexual fire has dwindled. They were just old and had no choice in the matter, so you thought.

Now, there are young couples, middle-age couples, blacks, whites, crossing all racial barriers, and elderly couples who still should be able to get their groove on but don't, erererer! An estimated 113 million or 15% and growing according to *"Newsweek Magazine" article dated June 30, 2003.* Doesn't it just give ya the shivers? This could be happening to your children, parents, grandparents or extended family members. Hey, don't think it's just happening to females. Males are snatched into it; however, a brother ain't too quick to admit it.

The purpose of this book is to draw awareness to the reality of what is going on (or not going) in the bedrooms of some marriages of the 21st century. It will also bring attention to a neglected issue that will empower couples to:

- Identify
- Clarify
- Confront
- Outsmart

the problem of living without sex in a marriage.   If these components are activated, then married couples can avoid these components:

- Heartaches
- Pain
- Trauma
- Frustration
- Loneliness

This book is not meant to bash husbands or belittle wives, nor any race, religion, culture, sexual orientation or lifestyle. It is to help those couples who are struggling with this issue become aware that they are not alone.   They too can come out of the closet.   They should not have to experience the absence of sex occasionally, or none at all, which is part of the marital union. Although making love is much more than the sexual act itself, wouldn't a spouse think that this was one of the greatest benefits of being married?

Well, couples don't have to sit idly by and settle for this

lifestyle. It just ain't natural. It takes more than a-hoping, a-coping, and a-praying. They need to know that they can make an effort to take action and find a solution or some alternative solutions, wise counsel, and peace in the midst of a sexless marriage (Philippians 4:7). Couples can also find spiritual answers and examine how the Gospel message bears upon this issue. If couples do decide to settle for such a lifestyle, they should get informed from articles, talk shows and books that relates to their situation.

For many, the church is the rock that anchors our lives and the place we can run to when all hell is breaking loose and we just ain't got no mo' juice to go on. Because so many of us look to churches for direction and guidance for life's challenges, we can come out of shock or disbelief by acknowledging that the issue of sex-less-ness exist, not just Bible stories of Hosea and Gomer (Hosea 1:2-3). Could it be possible that some churches don't want to be forthright in coming out publicly and would rather "stay stuck silently regarding sex in any form or fashion because of the embarrassment, confusion and shyness of the subject?" According to a book written by the marital expert, Dr. Miles Munroe, studies and other research, "they suggest it to be a personal or private social issue that is not adequately *spiritual*," for the Church." Isn't this astonishing? Wouldn't one think "that they would be the ones to become knowledgeable and confident and willing to come out of the closet because they follow God who is the creator of everything, including sex according to this book?" Yes, the Church might be saying "that these issues and lifestyles are more nontraditional than it has ever seen or heard of in the past;" but, these are complicated, real issues, nonetheless.

Maybe you are in a sexless crisis that was initiated by unexpected events such as infidelity, biological and physical challenges, sicknesses and diseases; or by a long, slow buildup of resentments and unresolved problems. Because of the lack of tolerance, understanding and communication; now your sexless marriage is having you contemplating a separation or a divorce.

I hope that this book will inform, educate, impact, inspire, uplift, entertain and provoke husbands and wives of every color, creed and age to *reevaluate* your commitment of your marital vows to God first. Secondly, each other and then allow Him to build your foundation on Godly principles to make a happier, healthier and intimate marriage. I also challenge you to lay aside the bickering and work hard to keep the flames flickering in your marriages. Learning to show *appreciation, complimenting* or *validating* one another and "yes," this could put the living libido loco back, without the axe in your bedrooms, if you so desire.

INTRODUCTION

Whether single, married, separated, or divorced, this book will offer you crisp golden nuggets, simple principles of real life, encouragement and truth about sexless issues. My desire is for you to make better decisions or choices in making your relationship more agreeably satisfying, fulfilling and rewarding.

Take this journey into Chapter 1, *HELLO, I'M MARRIED* and explore the {memories} of the way marriages once were. Love or lust was so simple then. Thought we really had comprehended!

CHAPTER ONE

HELLO, I'M MARRIED

One would assume as newlyweds, they had just begun a marriage made in heaven. You know how it was: So in love they thought they would die if they couldn't be together twenty-four/seven. Couples tend to be so tight; you couldn't run a pin thru em'. Laughing, giggling, holding hands, kissing, all the major fireworks! Couldn't wait to get home to get in the sheets! Hanging all over each other with so much love or lust in their eyes, that those looking on had to repent of being jealous or envious!

Yes, it started out that way, just like any married and passionate couple, in the sheets with fine body parts, biceps and triceps that would set your soul afire. The magic was just there. Your boo would say: "Come on baby light my fire." "Let's get it on…ooh baby. Let's get it on. (Mr. Marvin Gaye) There's nothing wrong with me loving you, hmnn…cause we're legally true, (have a license) yes we do, do, do!"

Keeping it on the real: most of the sistas, especially if they married young, thought the sun rose and shined on their husbands! You couldn't tell a sista nothing' about her man. She would be ready to scratch your eyeballs out and give a beat down to any sista who dared to step up to him. **Back-in-the-day**, if they would really tell the truth and shame the devil; they didn't have a clue about married life. That was what everybody else was doing. Some did it to escape their home environment, and others did not want to be labeled "an old maid." Quite a few did not want to abide by so-called "strict rules", so they married to spite their parent/s. They would just figure it out as they strolled along the course of their marriage. Some of their generation of parents didn't know about healthy, solid relationship skills either. If they did, I don't believe many would have settled for miserable, unproductive, unfulfilling and abusive lifestyles (physically or mentally).

Now, there were some sistas fortunate enough to have a storybook (Cinderella) wedding and others who could just barely get by with just the used ribbons, hand-me-down flowers, borrowed dress, and limited food, if you know what I mean. Marriage Counseling! What was that? Those that did, still did not consistently put it into practice. They must have drifted off. Someone forgot to yell "*wake up and pay attention*." Otherwise, we would not be battling with the overwhelming fifty percent or more divorce rate that is so prevalent in the church arena as well as the secular world.

On the up and up: For many, marriage was mainly the images that was portrayed on television shows and soap operas, such as, "As the World Turns." In which a sista's world would be turned upside down only to get to Church to be preached right side up again, because of some negative perception of the sistas having an overly aggressive "chip on their shoulders." Some really were captivated by "All My Children" because children were plentiful in most households; therefore, visiting "Generally Hospital" frequently! Then, we needed some "Days [to] Our Lives" and hoped "Guiding Light" would guide us to a place of serenity. What family of any ethnicity could measure up or relate to shows such as "Leave It to Beaver", "Father Knows Best", "I Love Lucy", "The Walton's", "The Brady Bunch", and "Little House on the Prairie" in which an unbalanced reality of the "perfect family syndrome" was displayed? Others had watched their parents, grandparents and other couples in and outside the church (the ones they perceived as having mature marriages). Marriage to some was sex, children, living paycheck to paycheck, struggling, juggling, tiresome or draining, sacrificing and trying to meet the bills and take their pills.

Do you find it disturbing that things haven't changed much in this millennium? Society is glorifying, idolizing, reinforcing and perpetrating what marriages and relationships should be through **some** unrealistic images of reality T.V. shows, sitcoms, entertainment magazines, books, movies, Hollywood media entertainment network, twenty-four-hour soap operas and gossip columns. For many couples, marriage is occasional sex, if any at all. They have living arrangements for convenience, mo' pills and alcohol to numb the void feelings of frustration, depression, loneliness and exhaustion. A lot of church marriages are running toe-to-toe with the secular pertaining to divorce. Some are wondering "are some churches conforming to the world's standard of a marriage (the kind that ya' chase em' and replace em')?"

Many couples have discovered that their marriage has gone through a time travel, (been processed, refined, stretched, fried, and parched). They have come to the realization that marriage falls under three stages: lust, cuss and fuss. Marrying immaturely, without having the proper knowledge (being uninformed), and having an unbiblical and unbalanced foundation are what lead to these realizations.

Are you on the hit list in Chapter 2 *"No Marital Sexual Bliss"*? And, you really don't have a clue or in denial as to why this might be so!

CHAPTER TWO

NO MARITAL SEXUAL BLISS

"Naturally the union of two unique, distinct personalities will sometimes entail challenging moments, conflicts incompatibilities, annoying habits, personal weaknesses, levels of stress or power struggles that they will have to deal with" according to the marriage expert Dr. Munroe. God bless the few who don't, but either way it goes; some will find that they are going to need a renewal of commitment, reevaluation, or an upgrade to their vows. A *couple's approach or response* in dealing with each category mentioned above *perhaps could affect the foundation of their relationship.*

A lot of couples, Christians or Non-Christians are mostly miserable. Downgrading a lifestyle that they have become accustomed to is hard to let go and ain't easy, especially after a mediocre one. Some men would say "it's cheaper to keep her." Nay, a sista says "it's convenient to keep him." They have too much invested and they might as well stay. Also some spouses don't want their children' lives uprooted and shattered. Lifestyles would change if divorce is mentioned! The finances would be limited. Especially when one spouse was issuing major duckies [dough]! Ya' know how it would be. Half of everything! Home-girls, we know half sometimes don't mean half. States can vary on the value of distribution. Home girls just ain't quick to change a lifestyle.

When they think of:

- the freaking mortgage, alimony
- child support
- baby mama drama, stepparent/stepchild drama
- then there's court cost; lawyer fees; judgment decrees
- visitation rights
- dividing property

and it becomes an ongoing saga...hey just forget it. Singing to Al Green's tune, "Let's Stay Together, Whether Good or Bad, Happy and Sad"! Phew! Give me a chill pill, and tell me what's not real. Now you can say what you have always wanted to say, "Cal-gon...take me away"!

Unfortunately, a lot of the men wanna break up the mundane. They start feeling like they have needs for an outlet. Yet, they won't go and talk to Kane; they go and play with Jane! See somebody new and if they don't be careful, their butts gonna catch the shoe from their wife with strife and a knife. Meow!

Because some husbands can't relate, they date and indulge themselves into numerous affairs, some serious and others not so serious. Wives are too caught up into:

- managing a job
- raising and hauling the children to soccer practice, baseball and football practice, piano and ballet lessons, karate lessons
- since the popularity of "Tiger-mania" and tennis sisters' pros "Venus and Serena Williams" [hauling them to golf and tennis lessons has become a top priority]
- household chores, help with homework, grocery lists, making sure the bills get paid, emotional and physical stress

and marital strife to give much attention to their sex life. Later they gasp and collapse into bed saying nothing. *Now*, what little sexual intimacy they had, have gone from barely existence to none. This lack has some screaming a couple of months/years later to the song "Get Me Out Jesus", by the outstanding songbird Valerie Boyd. How could this ever have happened?

Like the legendary Elvis Presley's song says "I'm all shook up." The boat has been rocked baby and like the one and only King of Blues, Mr. B. B. King can sing, "The Thrill is

Gone." Now, the chill is on! They are living without Niagara and Viagra. No living libido loco, none, nada! *No sexual bliss*! Girl friend has just gone cold turkey on the brother. Especially if he is continuously cheating! A sista says "you can't have your cake and pie too, and I ain't going nowhere!"

Although some husbands would frown at the idea of no-sex and because of their religious belief of no-divorce… "til death do us part", they would start new lives in separate households indefinitely. Therefore, some continuing their philandering, nonetheless still married in name only. Would this mean "sex on life support" for some wives? What about the others who spouses left and refused to have kept the vows when one became ill… "in sickness or in health"; however, the abandoned partner remains celibate and is hoping for the return of the spouse that has defaulted? Unimaginable, yet there are some in same households, but separate bedrooms or same bedrooms abstaining without the sex due to cheating spouses. You could categorize them in "Ripley's Believe It or Not" and society have forgot about them. Yet, they do exist.

NO-SEX! "I'm the man, and surely that can't be the plan" a brother gone shout! A sista say, "Is it just my imagination, once again, running away with me?" You know how our folks talk about ya'. They're gonna holler at you girl, as though you've developed a plague epidemic. They will say "it's something wrong with that picture." I guess you can't blame em', cause this sounds like some messed up crap that folks will flap their mouths about. Could this really be the norm in any committed relationship of any race? If it is, who is willingly going to fess up? Sometimes when you tell the males that you are sexless, some might say "don't play, cause I'm willing to lay with you." In addition, the females' response might be "if you ain't gay, you can have all this fillet mignon." As many will discover in another chapter, for some it is a choice and others it is not. It's no wonder many would rather stay in the closet! Who wants to be criticized, scrutinized, ostracized, or any other "*ized*?" You...? Me...? Who...?

See if you can agree if Chapter 3 "Real Issue: Cheating Spouses" can explain why there is no sexual flame because someone became untamed by another's flirtatious game. So, some can't pry between the thigh!

CHAPTER THREE

REAL ISSUE: CHEATING SPOUSES

Obviously, for some couples it will become self-evident, and for others their perspective of the root causes for their sexless marriage will lend itself to self evaluation, extensive soul searching and much needed time. As they peel back the layers, they are bombarded with thoughts of, *"what are the causes of this sexless lifestyle?"* Could the underlying scenarios include the following:

"All of your spending has put us deeper in the hole and the strain has taken a toll on our love life."; "I know you gotta work and bring home the bacon, but that demanding job have you spending too much time at that office and I'm left alone with these kids...tired of it"; "I was healing from the first affair, your straying again is delaying our sex life indefinitely"; "Isn't it obvious that we don't have anything in common and we're drifting further apart?"; "Our busy workload don't allow us to go anywhere or do anything together anymore...something gotta give!"; "When was the last time you paid any real attention to me and our sex life...why don't you visit the doctor"?; "I'm not attracted to you anymore"; "You know those kids might be listening...even if the door is closed!; "Honey you always gotta headache...what's really going on?" Does this sound to familiar?

Furthermore, other numerous suggested factors that have led to this dilemma in several articles titled *"Hopeful Solutions for Your Sexless Marriage"* written by Dr. Andrew D. Atwood and research by Dr. Jennifer Berman [director of the Female Sexual Medicine Center at UCLA Medical Center in Los Angeles] are:

"Biological challenges [interrupted challenges with your body or your partner]

- erectile dysfunction (which is commonly called impotence in men), low sexual desire, premature ejaculation, energy levels
- female hormonal imbalance, fibroids, cyst and tumors...and vaginal dryness that make it difficult to engage well sexually, menopause, thyroids, infertility, surgeries, birth control pills, post-pregnancies,
- severe vaginismus, hormone levels can sometimes drift dramatically due to things like childbirth, menopause and depression or hysterectomy, etc.

- problems with orgasms, lubricating, medical and chronic illnesses…issues in men and women such as diabetes, stroke, heart attack, high and low blood pressure, low or high libido/sex drives, medications, weight issues, kidney, liver, arthritis, Parkinson's, Aids, Cancer, Hypoactive Sexual Desire (HSD), etc.

"Personal and emotional challenges [emotional problems or external influences]

- unexpected life mishaps that leads some to eating disorders, financial matters, children, grief issues, poor body image
- rape and molestation, physical, mental and sexual abuse [the resulting shame, guilt, depression, and rage sometimes destroys trust and prevent intimacy and sexual pleasure]

"Cultural challenges [dealing with your beliefs in religion, ideas, morals or ethics that may differ from spouse, etc]

- "interracial or mixed marriages is not to be compared with mixed marriages of Jewish men marrying pagan and idolatrous women…Ezra 10." "This stand against "interracial marrying" should not be confused as ethnically based or race related, but rather as spiritually incompatibility" according to the marriage expert Dr. Miles Munroe.

"**Relationship Challenges** [lack of or non-communication…bad experiences from past relationships that haven't been dealt with]

- partner struggling with pornography or sex addiction, alcohol or drug addiction, gambling addiction, veteran servicemen and servicewomen struggling with post-traumatic stress disorder, depression, (antidepressants often affect sex drives), a nervous breakdown, stress.

- sexual boredom, sexual dissatisfaction, spouse on the down low or low down, sexual anxiety that hinders performance, negative conflicts from unresolved or unexpressed feelings of anger or resentment and

- rejection…about household duties, past actions, past arguments, maturity or immaturity level, avoidance of sexually transmitted diseases, avoiding conception...form of birth control, imprisonment...no visitation, stepchildren or extended family

- adultery can cause the partner having the affair to slow or stop sex with their partner, the victim of the affair refuses to have sex with the adulterer...often struggling mentally about the affair.

Although the current media blitz have reported problems/matters of this nature in *Newsweek Magazine* article titled: *"We're Not in the Mood: For married couples with kids and busy jobs, sex just isn't what it used to be. How stress causes strife in the bedroom—and beyond"*, by Kathleen Deveny...dated June 30, 2003. The author of *The Sex-Starved Marriage* by Michele Weiner Davis wrote that "low sexual desire/low sex drive" in men was the No. 1 complaint brought to sex therapists and other articles also emphasized that "sheer busyness of couples' jobs/careers/lifestyles and overwhelmed by the "B" word; (too *busy* working; too *busy* commuting to work; too *busy* hauling kids around to different activities; and too *busy* for sex [leading to exhaustion]"; is one of the top priorities of not connecting in the sack.

Nevertheless, many spouses believe that "the ***real culprit*** to this *sexless lifestyle* in most marriages is the issue of *infidelity* or *adultery*." Many couples are finding themselves unable and unwilling to commit and be faithful to their covenant vows. Can you reflect and travel down memory lane to the much publicized celebrities, evangelicals, priests, presidents or athletes and coaches caught in infidelity and sexual scandals over the past month(s), year(s) and decades? What about the ones that are kept hush-hush and out of the limelight? Just look around your own back yard or community.

According to Dr. Robin L. Smith, the #1 *New York Times Bestseller* author of (*Lies at the Altar: The Truth about Great Marriages*), "they lied at the altar in upholding their commitment to the vows without truly comprehension of the sacredness of the marital union." Especially marrying young, they feel "it is almost impossible to cherish the idea of having sex with only one partner for the rest of their marriage." Somehow they are convinced that the grass is greener and worth gazing. Marriage to some is like a buffet eatery. They have a choice of sampling and eating every food on the menu. Some men and women feel the need of desiring something different. Entangling themselves with a new body type or another set of lips seems refreshing at that moment. Oh what a web they weave and become deceived! The reality show "Cheaters" attest to this very notion. It is astonishing that in 2003, the Ashley Madison Agency, "A Web Site for Married People Looking to Have an Affair" had 50,000 members. What's more alarming is that in 2007, it had more than 1.2 million members.

A wife might not have an ounce of proof of her husband cheating, but the reason is that some are just so clever, smooth, secretive, and skillful with "their" wrongdoings.

However, some wives have what they call "women intuition". They just know what their husbands are up to because they had stopped satisfying them in the bed a long time ago. Moreover, if the truth is told; their "love-making" has gone from vivacious to starvacious. They just sense that they are going somewhere putting the *weenie in the bikini.* Therefore, a wife knows as high natured, passionate, scrumptious of a lover (and one who could make you exhale after the "love-making") as her man is; **could not go *without sex*** week *after week*, lately *month after month* and *year after year.* Oh no! Not a physically able man. Normally, a brother giving up sex is like taking away his BMW. Child Please!

Wives obviously know of their husbands' promiscuous behavior because of the visible trail of evidence the "other woman" leaves behind, such as:

- lipstick left in the husband's car that you know is not

yours

- a pair of earrings
- panties/thongs under the seat or in the bedroom
- photographs of your spouse with her
- hotel receipts
- cigarettes that obviously belong to another because the wife is not a smoker, etc.

Wives are sometimes silent and hope for the best or just let it rest. On the other hand, they turn a blind eye and a deaf ear. On occasion, the other woman will show up at the doorstep or the office. In addition, some husbands just confess after becoming overwhelmed with the guilt of leading a double life.

Somehow some wives discover that their men folk don't just cheat on them with one woman…depending on the "mind-set," it could be multiple people (sex orgies or group sex) at one time. Yeah, it ain't the norm now. Fasten your seat belt because anything can be expected now in this generation. We are living in perilous times according to 2nd Timothy 3:1-3; in which some humans are having illicit sex with animals. This is termed "bestiality". Some are also having sex with life-sized dolls (which some suggest was created for the purpose of replacing humans)! Then there's cyber sex! What else?

Although it is implied that some men are tempted to cheat

more often than women; new studies are revealing that "some women are becoming aggressively engaged in affairs as well." Who is to say that a lot of them weren't creeping back then, since no one was really keeping any statistical account? Because of their high salary jobs, they ascertain that they can pay to play. Who would ever have thought this? Remember the show: "It's A Different World"! Because of the feminist movement, some women feel equal to men...and want to do anything a man can do. Welcome to "This Millennium!" If you think *they* are stunned about it, how about this society? They certainly don't want this secret to come out of the closet because of their "machismo".

The Heart and Soul Magazine dated February and March 2008 has an article titled "Workplace Cheating". It asks the question, "Are you having an emotional affair? An "emotional affair" or an "affair of the heart" is the term society calls it. They emotionally cheat with an "office worker", an online chat room lover, or unconsciously some will attach themselves to an ex. Although there is no physical intimacy, they are enticed by the secrecy and deception", according to the article.

Since there are no reliable statistics on how many affairs are exclusively sexual or emotional; most experts say, "Women are more likely to choose emotional affairs...a potentially romantic connection that does not include sex…than men." "The discovery that the emotional betrayal or the breach of trust, sometimes rather than the act of the sex itself becomes the most painful aspect of the affair is quite surprising to many. It also can seem like the most difficult to recover from", according to some therapists.

Most wives are usually forgiving about the betrayal of the first affair. The reason being…"when a woman loves a man-love deserves another chance", they will say. No wonder *inquiring minds would love to know, "why are some spouses/partners not denying the* cheater, deceiver the "*cookie*"? Her bond is just too much of a good thang to let him go. A one-time fling does not make one a throw away, should it? Isn't there a difference between an affair and a fling? In all honesty, it is suggested that "some men on the other hand are usually not so forgiving. They will pack and go a-living elsewhere." This false sense of their perception of love eludes them into the belief that they have to save face and not be the victim of cheating. They make the decision of beating their "so called beloved" physically and quite often becoming a fatality. This leads to another "domestic violence" issue.

However, hats off to some real men who ain't stunned and choose not to run, even though they might be disgusted when their ladies get busted. Moreover, far too often, some men are dishonored…sometimes labeled "henpeck" when they choose not to leave the nest and want what's best for their children and for some *their marriage.* "Take A Bow"!

Obviously, research has revealed, "some women don't know a good man when one is staring them in the face."

Some spouses want to believe that their marriage has a chance after infidelity. What's that saying, "everything worth having is worth fighting for?" Remember the song "Love the One You're With" by the late, soulful "Mr. Luther Vandross"! "Finding another partner who has the same potential to cheat might be risky anyway", some will say. Would not one think it is easier to recover the wreckage in this relationship and focus on the positive aspects that they share and strengthen it?

Remember the phrase "I Can't Believe It's Not Butter"; some would say "I Can't Believe They Didn't De-clutter" from *sexual escapades* after infidelity. Some studies have suggested that "they would rather forgive and live on purpose and move forward or either in a state of denial or request that the mess is left alone." Remarkably, some don't have a clue that they don't have to do the do (*give up the cookie*), when their significant other *screw* up. Especially a serial cheater! They have a *choice*! It's embedded in their psyche because some preachers teach that it's their God given duty to perform no matter what was done.

Now, the wife strives to give the marriage her utmost attention because she feels she can resolve any challenge that confronts or becomes a threat to their bond of matrimony. She starts strategizing new ways to try and spice up the romance by: a) cooking gourmet meals by candlelight b) re-styling hair weekly c) acquired new or rearranged wardrobe d) arranged monthly date nights e) weekend getaways f) walks at the park or beach and g) spontaneity sex [quickies] etc. She studies as if she is enrolling in a course titled: "Survival of the Fittest" (Ways to Keep Your Man Satisfied). Sista girl is on an all out mission. Home girls are wondering what's up? No time for the sistas----- no shopping, no aerobic workouts, no movie nights, broad-way plays, or dining and wining. You know; all that fun stuff...Girl's Night Out! A circle of women discovers that despite efforts of:

- modeling the new skimpy
- sexy gowns, thongs, {which is sometimes unbearable} from Victoria's secret
- playing Jayne {swinging from the bedroom pole}
- getting the blouses showing your cleavage
- challenging partner with new sexual positions and places
- putting on the skirts [some go as far as putting on

the daisy dukes]

- attempting to be Miss Play Wife of the day, month, and year, only to come back down to planet Earth to be ignored and humiliated!

They realize that no matter what they do to enhance the marriage,...more intimacy, caretaking, and more sex, some husbands are still not satisfied, continuously curious or adventurous (straddling the fence), and obviously and sometimes blindly cannot see the treasure within you.

Wives are baffled and pondering over the question concerning their men folks as to "Why can't they get no satisfaction?" They say to themselves, "What's the use?" "I'm the only one trying to acquire self-help materials to repair and rekindle the flame and finding myself once again settling to be tamed by my adulteress partner!" "This marriage seems to be one-sided" "I seem to be the only one loving unconditional." Are men too at ease in Zion? Do they not have the same drive women possess to work on the marriage? Sadly enough some women/wives were already feeling unappreciated, unsupported and overworked. These negative thoughts will have quite a few wallowing in self-pity. Is this the reason they go "Looking for Mr. Good-bar", "The Clean-up Man" or "Jodi"?

Uh huh! The men are saying, "What about me? I am

disciplined and committed enough to not roam. I got her a nice home; a top of the line phone and she's living in the A-zone. Sure, my humanistic side may have had me foaming at the mouth occasionally for "The Clean-Up Woman...that song by deep down rooted soulful Ms. Betty Wright!" Yet I chose not to cross that line even though it becomes obvious that it will cost you a fine. So what's up with her?

Sadly, the majority of the time it has nothing to do with you. Didn't ya know, *"Men are from Mars and Women are from Venus* (LOL) according to author John Gray. And could it be that they are of the *dog/she-dog species*? Studies have suggested that "it's about their need to fulfill their inadequacies or insecurities. That insecurity can be about their job or their sexuality, etc." Or, past issues and hurts that have not been healed or dealt with. Face facts please, some women need a reason and men just need a place, lol. A man's reasoning is that "once sex is initiated, orgasm/pleasure/relaxation is sure to happen." In addition, some women are magnets to what many refer to as "the bad boy syndrome". They tend to find good guys boring; so they go soaring. They fail to realize that after they experience living in the fast lane, there true good thang has caught a plane to "Sane Island". Every thang is over!

According to the bestselling author, Michael Baisden's

book "Never Satisfied: How and Why Men Cheat", it suggests that in the *ruthless game of cheating*; "there are no romantic conclusions or happy endings; only rude awakenings; and hard lessons". *Cheating* ain't easy, no one gets any pleasing out of it. The onset fixation is only for a duration and what felt charming eventually becomes harming to both spouse, children and others involved. *Infidelity* is a no win-win situation. It can drain you mentally, physically and more than likely it will drain your pocketbook/wallet. Are you aware of the addictive forming behavior that can occur? Check out the bible story of "Sampson and Delilah"! You might say he was smitten by love or lust and addicted!

After discovering that your spouse has cheated, waste no time in denying that this has happened. CONFRONT: don't bury your head in the sand. Otherwise it will land you in a firestorm of inconceivable disaster and devastation. The other woman plots and feels that she can undermine your husband/man because of your non-combative or nonchalant response. The presumption that he has gotten you…the wife under control due to the fact that he's successfully fulfilling a lifestyle of singleness with her! He is continuing to spend three or four nights a week with her! Therefore, her planned pregnancy that you were suspicious of has become a reality and a nightmare for your family. Let's face it; some of these mistresses main objective is to use the baby as a lottery ticket. Especially if he's wealthy, has his own business, or has a great paying job…they view this as hitting the jackpot. Is this to suggest that he and his family are being pimped by the mistress?

Whenever you decide to face the hurdle of infidelity, either way your feelings may have your emotions reeling erratically, so step back and reassess. *Listen to their words carefully*! Take this moment to reevaluate if he/she is sincerely capable of *desiring* to change. Rearrange your schedule to get couple therapy. Talking about things when you are both in a calm and rational state becomes beneficial. Therefore, not rehearsing the blame game and talking openly. If not, another lesson learned from the "school of hard knocks" and you don't let it block your progress. When they continue in their cheating, fleeting ways, for some this could be where the rubber meets the road. It also could be "the straw that breaks the camel's back and there a** gonna or should lack." Tell a brother or a sista "don't play." You are not Burger King, and they can't have it their way when they are dethroned and wrong. Better yet, are they trying to have their cake and pie too? Some might be thinking "Hit the Road Jack" by the legendary Ray Charles. Or, as the *"King of Pop*, Mr. Michael Jackson express in his song "Beat It".

However, it is important to note that no matter how doom and gloom things might be after an affair; your marriage still can make a change to rearrange and bloom according to the books *"The Divorce Remedy and Divorce Busting,"* written by Michelle Weiner Davis. The healing will involve some kneeling and forgiveness. Some therapists believe "that the both of you must become fully committed and do what it takes to get back on track" although you might be without the knick knack for a minute. Knick knack pat-a-wack can't give that dog/she dog a bone (cookie)…this old/young man or woman can't come rolling home (remix of a nursery rhyme lol)! Others say, "You can get the ball rolling alone, starting out". Sometimes *alone* counseling can be a bonus. It can help you take stock and sort out the dilemma of the affair or issues. For so many, the recovery process can take years…don't expect a quick fix solution from the repercussion of an affair. *When the two of you obviously can't get a grip*, tip your fingers to the yellow pages. Pave it forward by looking into couple's therapy, family counseling and sex therapy.

In this millennium of increased knowledge and technology, if people are exploring and going to tennis, golf, baseball or football clinics to improve their game, seeking therapy or counseling for resolution to marital issues might deem to be productive. How about a clinic for teaching males "how not to cheat"? Better yet, a Life Class course that entails a learning skill to be "faithful". Also, consulting a doctor to spot-check to see if there may be a medical reason behind your dissatisfaction with your sex drive! There are no excuses; you can Google everything if you have access to a computer. The library grants you a certain amount of time if you don't have one in your home. Better yet, your bookstore armed with a web of information waiting for you to embark upon! Studies are revealing "that there may be alternative drugs for depression and other conditions that can have less of an impact on your sex drive." Research suggests "that poor health is inhibiting male and female sex drives." You could imagine that good health practices resulting from an increased and proper or improved diet and exercise can help restore one's libido.

For many they can say "bye bye to yesteryears of embarrassing awkward penile pumps, implant surgery, unappealing suppositories, questionable herbs, and even less appealing ejections," that was used for resurrecting blood supply to the penis to sustain an erection. No longer do some men have to suffer from ED (Erectile Dysfunction). A certain amount of ladies might say "hip hip hooray" for the miraculous blue pill "*Viagra*" which was the first to appear on the scene. *Cialis,*

Levitra and V-Mack...these are other well known erectile dysfunction drugs that have come on the scene. Some articles suggest "that they may work pretty consistently and safely—not for everybody, but for many". Obviously, men must have a death wish....they are interchangeably using someone else's Viagra pills. A big no-no...an early grave! **Always consult your physician before use of any drugs or any medication**.

Chapter 4 will tell you more about the Church body; your body; somebody, and the busy bodies intermingling with everybody.

CHAPTER FOUR

WHOSE BODY IS IT ANYWAY?

The scripture tells you that "Marriage is honorable among all, and the bed undefiled" (Heb. 13:4). Yes, and you know that's suppose to be the truth! You're saying "this marriage thing works both ways." A husband should keep his body under subjection as well as a wife. Woe, the Spirit is willing, but the flesh (body) is weak. (Matthew 26:41) The flesh is always at war with the spirit. Get Real:----times out of----some (church men or ungodly men) bodies are every which way but subjecting! This is not to suggest that they can't. An urgency of training men to control their body is what's needed.

Don't act like this does not happen. Y'all know how some eyes pop and can't stop gazing and dazing and zoom in on the voluptuous "Butt Sisters" that strolls the walkway to the offering table. The "Breasted Sisters" are not far from view. The majority of men are very visual. There's a saying "it might be tight but its' right!" Everybody's mind ain't regenerated and transformed. A lot of y'all ain't totally set free and delivered from your past, or is it still your present? Sure! Your spirit man got saved but your flesh did not (unless God instantaneously did surgery and purged you). Walking out your process of salvation is your part.

Because of the myth that "there is a male shortage," some women become desperate. Seeking any able bodied male that they feel is available or not available. They forgot every moral standard their mama and papa ever taught them about dating somebody else's husband or man. In addition, there are those male species that go a panting after a man's wife; just because of the challenge that she's forbidden territory (although they are conscious of the fact that there are plenty of available singles). Something about the chase presumably!

On occasions, they can lose all senses of reality and become obsessed stalkers. Has anybody met that kind? Before ya know it, their bodies become too entwined. Females become obsessive and possessive over them and begin to spoil them a lot too. Some literally pay them to be with them. Physically fight over 'em too! If the shoe fits, ya just say "ouch!" Mostly everybody has played the fool sometimes. The competition and rivalry come into play with the wives and other female counterparts. The man can't help but to take it all in stride. The attention makes him delusional in thinking that "he's bodylicious".

He's pounding his chest and saying "he's the man." Yes, they are rooting him on and want him to be the man and the king of his castle or home *until the queen arrives.* Did not James Brown, the godfather of soul try to tell you in his song "It's a Man's World?" But we females can agree "that it wouldn't be nothing; without a woman or a girl."

Some of this attention makes some men become to body image conscious. They express the "it's all about me attitude." Did not their brains possibly register the difference between selfishness and having self-interest? Yes, it is wise and intelligent to be interested in yourself. Some just go to the extreme with it. (Leviticus 19:18 NIV) says "Love your neighbor as yourself." If you don't like you, obviously how could you possibly like your neighbor? And then there are others…especially women, who don't take out any time for themselves. They are always putting others above themselves at any cost. Are these the ones who do not know how to say "no" and their bodies shut down?

So much of this "self body image vanity concept" is wreaking havoc among spouses and they become bruised emotionally and physically. When they get up enough nerves and air their issues or complaints to their pastor/clergy, family or friends about their discontentment…the body of Christ tells wounded brothers and sisters to:

- "Hold on till a change comes , it will happen after awhile"
- "God doesn't put no more on you than you can bear
- "What doesn't kill you strengthens you"
- "Weeping may endure for the night but joy cometh in the morning"
- "An old church mother might say: baby, Shh! don't tell anybody"
- "Pray!" "It's gonna work out" , "it will be alright"
- "It's in his nature to cheat, boys will be boys, men will be men"
- "That's just the dog in him as long as he gives you respect"
- "As long as he's paying those bills putting a roof over yo head"
- "And ain't killing you stay with that man child!"
- "A piece of a man is better than no man who wants to be alone?"
- "You're the husband, you're supposed to hold the family together at whatever cost"
- "Give her time to mature, she will grow out of her childish ways"

- "You obey those that have the rule over you cause obedience is better than sacrifice, so you go home and submit to that man child"
- "You know you are your brother's keeper and the strong is to bear the infirmities of the weak"
- "Your body does not belong to you…that is your cross to bear"
- "No cross/no crown, keep hanging on in there"

Well! Some of these sayings may very well be true, but in the meantime…a body of believers and non-believers alike [those involved directly or indirectly] are in churches all across America. Sunday after Sunday, week after week, they are going through the motion and are {suffering} {growing weary} {frustrated} {angry} {fainthearted} {confused} {bewildered} {hurting} {depressed} {tormented} {bitter} {suicidal} and {at a loss of what to do} *in a marriage of betrayal, unhappiness, complacency; sex-less-ness and deceit.* They are literally dying in their circumstances and crying out, "HELP ME!" "What do you do, when you've done all you can and you did "Stand"…the song by Gospel Prodigy, Pastor Donnie McClurkin? What do I do during the Process of Waiting until the Victory or a Change Comes in this state of sexless-ness?

Because of the overwhelmed masses that are entering

mega churches, the leaders are engrossed in building larger buildings to accommodate the growing membership and sometimes don't get to address specific needs of the body as a whole. The churches addressing issues *obviously cannot carry the load alone.* A lot of times the media fail to recognize or give them enough exposure, if at all, for what they are doing.

The reality of some small Churches is that they don't have the resources, proper training, adequate facilities, financial funds and manpower to research or address the issue. Therefore, they are not making a significant cultural impact in resolving the breakdown concerning the critical issues of our day. This leaves perhaps many congregants in a state of unrest and perplexed. Therefore, some are exiting churches prematurely with minor transformation. Perhaps, this leaves some of them to even more "broke, busted, and disgusted", unbalanced, dysfunctional lifestyles! The roots of bitterness and offense engulf many and have some believing that the churches just don't care and are sweeping issues under the rug. Could it be possible that Churches have not effectively learned how to reach the Body of Christ?

Because of the uniqueness of this issue, the faith community should come together, brainstorm, and find out what is the church's role in addressing this. They could assist by researching, surveying and interviewing people who have experienced and struggled through these issues (ones who have not camped out in self-pity and received a transformation); have survived and are still sane and not ashamed to talk about their stories. Churches could present this issue in such a way that everyone might take heed! Most saints and sinners relate to plays, skits, movies, seminars, workshops, support groups and forums, etc. These might be great tools for dealing with this topic.

If they don't have the expertise, churches could direct them to some qualified, trained, licensed therapists or counselors. This of course, entails being in a Church that minister's aims to meet the person where he/she is in light of experience. In addition, there is a relationship system called "Marriage Fitness", an alternative to counseling. Warning: every counselor, therapist, sexpert or sex therapist, psychologist, sexologist, court-appointed therapist or family counseling, doctor, clergy or whomever your advisor, *does not always mean that their method works for you.* Ask questions and **check thoroughly** for specific training in an area of importance to your situation. Ex: Are they marriage friendly? Are they biased to the man or woman? Or, are they only echoing psychological "mumbo jumbo" and don't have a real clue about this issue? As only the beautiful and vibrant "Donna Summers" expresses in her song: *"You Work Hard for Your Money."* Cause time is money, so you need to get it right!

Yes, many of you are aware of the principle that "you all have no sole authority over your bodies when you marry" according to the Bible found in 1st Corinthians 7:4. It is scriptural [1st Corinthians 7:5] "that a husband and wife can bodily disconnect from sex when both spouses agree because of prayer and fasting or other reasons to their discretion." *What happens when the marriage bed becomes defiled?* One spouse commits the act of adultery. His/her body becomes one with a harlot. Are you aware that every person your spouse connects his/her body with...the residue of one's spirit is inside of you? "That person's body becomes a soul-tie with the two of you", according to the book "No More Sheets"! That relationship cannot easily be severed; therefore not allowing you to dismiss them so easily! When a husband/wife is making love, it is also with every other partner/s that they have had. Think about the time one partner or the other had shouted out someone else's name when ya'll was getting to the nitty gritty!

The question that some couples are struggling with is "Should they continue to submit their bodies to a defiler of the marital bed?" Sure, they are conscious of the fact that they have a legal right to divorce a spouse because of infidelity...Matthew 19:9; (yet many choose to remain and try to claim the victory regarding their plight and fight for their marital union). Some rationalize with the concept that "their bodies will eventually wind down with age." Surely, it can't jangle and dangle always. Moreover, after the hype, then you get to swipe all those cards. Lol!

Golden Nugget: Do you know if your body will be fit to handle the emotional and mental things that infidelity entails? Are you up to the challenge of being martyrs or super wives or super husbands and still remain submitted to the marriage after infidelity...especially if there was an unction in your spirit gnawing at you. Moreover, in your knowing, perhaps you should leave...if just for a season. Whether that unction was "His" *small still voice*, "His" speaking through a T.V. program, or could have very well been in a book or other ways. God is always communicating. It's always up to us to sit quietly or still to listen and observe. Watch as well as pray!

In the meantime, some of them who remained in their adulterous marriage and did not adhere to that unction, [are still miserable], and have died before time even after all of that submitting and self-sacrificing. Only to be mourned by the spouse a month, three months or six months, some may mourn you a year and then replace you with the hoochie momma or trick daddy that you tried your best to keep your spouse from. Some stories reported "that they neither wait until your body is cold in the ground; they go and hold your spouse's hand on the gravesite". You're dead at rest, in the sunset, and they are somewhere living peachy with Ms. or Mr. Teachy.

Please note that *God will honor the commitment to marriage in spite of infidelity.* According to some, "there are occasions when they felt led by God to stay in the marriage. And when God guides, "He" will provide," they will comment. For those who don't know whether they have heard from God or not, "He" will allow what you allow. "God's *grace* and *mercy* will have to be sufficient!" Sometimes reaping with mercy!

The news, movies, research and TV, etc exemplify some of the negativity when married folks go out there and have gotten their bodies entangled with another man or woman. Going out with a pout to prove a point, a lot of times backfire on you. What's fair for the goose ain't always fair for the gander 'cause they'll scandal your name and you are ashamed and still in pain. Although most men cheat sheet can be a mile long, some of our culture and church body sometimes give them many passes. Is this just? When it's all said and done and you feel conned, **seek God wholeheartedly** if you are to remain submissive sexually to your adulteress spouse.

Anyways, some spouses are putting their body in motion, putting their mind on alert that (with God's help, grace, and mercy), they plan to take control of their own body. The scripture says "work out your own salvation with fear and trembling" Philippians 2:12. Truth be told, you can't please everybody all the time. You gonna be criticized no matter what choices you make. Everybody is not in your corner, not happy for you and is not going to celebrate you. Don't get all bent out of shape even if it becomes church folks, family, friends and acquaintances. Some "so-called Christians do not have a *personal relationship* with our Almighty God. They are **religious**, therefore following **tradition** of men rather than God. The terminator (devil) don't care if it's the preacher or the teacher, nor the saint or the ain't. His aim is to make everybody's testimony look bad.

These earthen bodies possess humanistic characteristics that sometimes fall short of perfection…Romans 3:23.
Strive to live up to God's best standards. You just can't take it personally when somebody becomes vulnerable and falls prey to sin. Do not perpetrate a fraud as if you have been saved all of your life. Some of your saved selves are still struggling with some old issues you started with. Even with that said; don't let this be a handicap or an excuse to keep doing wrong things. Ya

know, when you *willfully* and *knowingly* continuing in your same old sin. Some might be thinking: God forgives you 7 times 77. But who really knows when that number is up for you? God knows the *intention of the heart.*

1st Corinthians 12:14 stresses that every part of the Church body needs the other, no matter how insignificant they think they are. No one part should be able to stand by itself. There is strength and unity in numbers.   Pray for synergistic divine connections. There are prayer phone lines if you do not want busy bodies in your business or affairs. This gives you the opportunity to connect with someone who has the skills to assist you in your time of need without the fear of someone sharing your personal information with others.

BEWARE! When some folks tell you, what they want or will not put up with! Believe it or not, some are putting up with a lot more than you are. It doesn't take a "rocket scientist" to look around and pay attention. You are darned if you do; you're darned if you don't. But, nobody is worth dying for. What good is an unhealthy body? Only "you" and God know when your body has had enough. "He want put no more on you than you can bear"; yet, he allows what you allow. Put it in survival mode before it takes a toll on you!

Golden nugget: plan your work and work your plan. Let

Go and Let God. 1st Peter 5:7 "Casting all your care upon him; for he careth for you." With all these incurable, untreatable diseases, one would think it would be wise to yield your body to Jesus Christ in fasting, prayer, and meditation? Only "He" can heal your spirit, soul, and mind. Think, Think, about what you might do to yourself! Your body really is precious and worthy of making a good investment in it. Why not?

Yep, a wife is still alive in Chapter 5 *"Help a Wife Out"*. Could you be the one in such a sexless life who is gliding, sliding or residing?

CHAPTER FIVE

HELP A WIFE OUT!

Believe a wife when she tells you that being sexless the majority of the time is not an easy choice. Let's get real here people. Do you think that any normal, baby making machine, coca cola bodied shape, mocha-skin-tone, highly sexual sista would want to stop getting her groove on and go cold---ole---ole---turkey on a brother in the sex department?

However, for one reason or another, some couples have been struggling with this (sexless issue) in the marriage for quite some time now. Can you imagine for some, it has been ten years? Yeah, you heard me right, *ten sexless years; for others five, four, three, two, one and some, a couple of months.* But no matter how astounding the numbers, this ain't supposed to be. Especially not for couples in the age groups of 21-70! Hmn Huh! Could this be you right now that's reading this book? Stuck in a sexless lifestyle! Too shame to admit, for fear of what your folks, friends and society is going to say.

A lot of wives say "that they've been up, down, in, out, and spun around long enough, wondering if they are to be forever the victim, and burden bearer of being the fix-it-woman, problem solver, door mat and web cobbler?" Seems to them, they might as well stay in the marital game and be hanged, than to be blamed for the failure of the relationship even at the sacrifice of being sexless. They feel it's their ultimate duty, or responsibility to work it out; if they don't, they are considered the bad, sad, nag, of a wife.

You, like some of these wives have been in this lifestyle for so long that you're saying "I might as well stick it out." Phew! "At least I know what I got and what I'm dealing with." "Even if the grass is greener; I ain't getting no younger and trying to learn another's habits take too much time and effort." "A piece of a marriage is better than no marriage at all and no man should be an island." "Cause starting over shole ain't easy!" "Just the thought of starting over surely has taken a bite out of me!"

I wanna be a queen and not mean, or a wife and not a knife. Is this what I've got to look forward to for the rest of my marriage? Not a desperate housewife, not a wife that's just starved for sex, but; I ain't made of stone either. I have desires and feelings. Still have hormones, and come-ons. I'm a compassionate, caring, passionate, productive, vibrant and creative human, made of flesh and blood. Amen. "S.O.S, 911!"

Chapter 6 *"Help A Husband Understand"*...although many conflicts and things are not quite grand, yet I still try to stand and be the man God created.

HELP A HUSBAND TO UNDERSTAND!

"Never thought in a million years this could have happened" says a loving husband. Especially being the "best man she had ever known!" "I did not give her any reason to roam." No one could have convinced me that I did not run a wonderful, satisfying home. Please, please tell me what went wrong? I'm trying to be strong! Haven't been the "cheating dog nor the selfish hog" that some have stereotypically labeled us.

She states that she would "beat me to the punch, before she would get debunched," even though she had no reason to be suspicious or any hunch of me being the cheater, the deceiver.

Trying to refrain from anger and remain calm. Do not want to be the forever sucka and pucka my lips. Trust is a must I know, but I'm not made of steel and need time to heal.

I'm another patiently waiting male that's experiencing a *drought* and trying not to pout. After two months/years or more of the lack of the sexual intimacy, don't you think it's time for her to be about her marital duties?

If the studies are correct that states "cheating has been

known to be the largest cause of divorce in the world history of mankind", and usually it's the man who's the chief offender of cheating. Can a wifey understand I'm purposely trying to avoid becoming another statistic?

If I'm willing, wouldn't you think she'd be living up to the expectancy of desiring to be in a monogamous relationship? Yea, yea, I'm aware of her will that is involved and God won't go against anyone's will. Can you blame me if I'm becoming ill at the dissatisfaction of not getting it on? She's the one that wanna roam.....and hell, if anybody should be angry....that's me.

Trying to lean and glean from the "good book" and not get hooked to the wrong things!

Can you possibly relate to Chapter 7 *"The Single"* who would mingle with Mr./Miss. Wrong...yet attempted to fix him/her into Mr./Miss. Right?

CHAPTER SEVEN

THE SINGLE

Before you hop off that train of singleness and try to get that ring to be entwanged by matrimony, as the Queen of Soul, Aretha Franklin says, "You better THINK about it!" You might need to have a flashback for a moment down memory lane. **Some** of you might remember that your parents, relatives and friends' marriages weren't all that. There were many catfights, sleepless nights, mark bites, bedroom brawls, police calls, and numerous couch let-outs. Yet, some remained and some rearranged themselves from all the theatrics that marriage can sometimes bring. Golden nugget: (Don't assume every relationship has to have drama to enhance a better union. You can *choose* to stay out of the madness).

So while you, as a single, have been itching to get hitched; you have the married trying to get ditched. Many of them are most miserable and feeling like they are living and experiencing Hell on Earth. With some couples, she is screaming "It's always your way." Then he'll yell "It's my way or the highway." No mutual agreement of getting each other's needs met. "A house divided cannot stand." Matthew 3:25.

Are you curious as to what a sexless marriage has to do with the single? Plenty! You have so many unmarried long and short-term couples/relationships that are experiencing the same sexless scenarios as the married, but without the legal benefits when it's all said and done. Ya know! "Shacking", "co-habitating", or "common-law marriage", are the terms being labeled. They are dealing with unnecessary plights such as *"having the thrills without the frills", or "not paying for the milk because they have the cow for free!", "getting the goods while you're in the hood" or "having a fling for many years with no ring!"*

Somehow the cleaning, the laundry, cooking, grocery shopping and the trash take out become routine. Does she/he not realize that they are acting out a spouse's role before time? Their names are omitted from the deeds, yet they are committed in paying the fees of utilities, insurance, rent or house note, and a car note while they're barely afloat (vice versa), etc. The moment challenges and heated fellowship/arguments confront them; they get upset and punish you by *withholding the money and the honey*. Phew! You're feeling heartbroken, rejected and abandoned and find yourself in an uncommitted sexless relationship. Some will eventually bailout without the payout.

Especially after signing a "pre-nuptial", they definitely won't let you forget the "*no-strings*" attached rule or "friends (without fringe benefits)." Unfortunately, many exit relationships with their finances whacked and not intact.

Before you say I do and remain true to your supposedly life partner, get *yourself* together first. Find out what's deeply rooted in you from childhood. What generational traditions or stereotypes were imprinted in your mind? Get all the quirks out. "*An ounce of prevention is worth a pound of cure.*" This is why communication, acquiring knowledge with a good understanding and pre-marital counseling before marriage is important. Tim, Jim and Slim, or Sue, Clarue, and Beverlue cannot make you whole after marriage. Maybe you won't have to scream, "I married an alien from outer space."

In order for you not to be alone, you can have enjoyable fellowship with friends or acquaintances. It does not have to be about a serious date to hook a mate. Hang out with family members or friends and go to social events, public gatherings and embrace other people and cultures. Forming sports' team, book clubs or participating in a single's support group or doing volunteer work should keep you from being too idle. Sometimes it is wiser and emotionally safer in numbers. The temptation of fornication can be lessened, hopefully. Would one not think it wise to seek singles that have common goals, (preferably drama free, financially free, emotionally baggage free)? Ex: "If one desire children and the other do not, don't waste valuable time?" "Is one too clingy and the other is the outgoing kind? Ex: "You expect his/her undivided attention at all times or one is always involved in something to do." "What if you're sexually conservative and they are a sex addict...once a week or every other week is enough for you but he wants it three (3) times a day?" "How will they spend their money? Ex: Will one spend excessively or the other stingily?" "How will one discipline the children? Ex: One might believe in spanking and the other might not!" Will he/she be committed to a monogamous relationship?

If life is about choice, choose what is right for you. Bad choices have unhealthy consequences. There are rewards when you make good choices. Certainly, upholding your virginity until marriage would be a great choice. Your virginity is a precious commodity. Once you leave the "Virgin" Islands (or you give it up), you have entered a blood covenant. Every person you sleep with afterwards is inside you. If you don't get purged mentally and emotionally from those individuals before marriage, you could be at the altar having flashbacks of them. Some of you might need X-ray vision to get back focused as to who you are supposed to be marrying.

THE SINGLE

Please note that everyone cannot remain single due to their own chemical makeup. Use discretion about the quote "that it's better to marry than to burn; *don't rush due to lust.*" Don't let society, family, friends, and peers pressure you about getting married. You can be happily single. However, if marriage is your desire, take into consideration whether you will allow your mate to influence or change your moral values. The question is, should your marital values be compromised? Beware: you might catch some flack from family members, friends or others that will assume that you might think you're better if you fail to lower your standards and not be willing to compromise your values or selections. However, the plumber, the mechanic, a contractor, the garbage man, or an insurance man, etc., should not be excluded in your selection of men. Quite a few make as much money as the doctor, the lawyer, an accountant or a dentist, etc. A little soap and water can do miracles. Are you like some who feel like it's a double standard when it comes to the brothers' dating outside their race? It's usually o.k. for them, but not a sista. Seeking individuals with the same morals or shared values (that are similar as possible):

- ❖ Dreams
- ❖ Beliefs
- ❖ Spirituality

❖ Similar interests or lifestyles

❖ Healthy respect for money

❖ Good work ethics

❖ Good credit and hopefully debt free

and one that has *integrity* and *respect* for you sounds like some wisdom along with commonsense. Some suggest that "you get specific with God as to what you desire in that person…down to the last detail." If you are not willing to share your time, privacy, material goods, some secrets, (some thangs you might not tell, they might bail, and send your tail in the mail with a nail), wallet/money, and make known or be held accountable for your whereabouts, then marriage might not be on your agenda at this moment. Pre-marital counseling is still not a guarantee that every marriage will last forever, but it certainly can't hurt. In addition, ongoing counseling sessions is a recommendation after the marriage. A financial advisor or planner certainly is worth looking into.

Just because someone's opinion that you value, tells you to hook-up with someone does not make him/her necessarily correct. Grow up and become the mature, creative, multitalented, purpose driven adult that you know that you can be. Read and seek wise counsel. If that inner unction inside of you is not making you feel right about *that* someone, you need to find out why? Remember the words of the single's specialist, bestselling author and speaker, "Michelle McKinney Hammond" honestly admitted, that "she (like all of us, has made classic mistakes)." Fortunately, she has lived and learned better. She has more than thirty (30) books under her repertoire that can help someone benefit from the relationship game and "you no longer have to play it by ear." See if her clear, practical incite of expertise can benefit you.

I hope that this book, "The Sexless Marriage" will at least provoke your thinking process; and, help you to avoid the traditional path of *dating and mating or struggling and juggling* needlessly when you do decide to wed. I also hope that you will try to avoid the constant power struggles, challenges or pitfalls, and unhappiness that even those in Christianity and those living outside of Christianity are facing in relationships; and that you will **gain knowledge**. *"The knowledge of the truth shall make you free"* and gain clarity to what a marriage truly should be according to the "manual"…the Bible. To the singles that have mingled and tingled, this chapter is certainly not to offend, condemn, criticize, or belittle you, mishaps or mistakes do occur. God always have an outstretched hand, a forgiving heart and the God of many chances.

Although there are some pre-and-post marital counseling

sessions, ministries dealing with singles and couples, be sure to **research them carefully**. A book titled *"Can I Really Be Stress Free"* poses a very interesting question. The book suggests that you can be stress free. You are truly are too blessed to be stressed! Pray for guidance. Do your homework singles!

Chapter Eight *"The Married"* will have carried some of you reading this section into an "aha" moment and you begin to wish you could *beam* yourself out of existence like Captain Kirk or Mr. Spock on the legendary show *"Star Trek"*. Then there are the others who can began to appreciate that their marriage might be great after all.

CHAPTER EIGHT

THE MARRIED

Whether you stumbled, fumbled or rumbled your way into it, marriage is still a God ordained institution between one man and one woman. It is a good idea and can be joyous, pleasurable and rewarding. Contrary to how it looks: a chaotic state of unrest, uncertainty, instability and an all out attack by the "Terminator (devil)". Remember that movie. It was about a machine that was destroying everything in its path. The Church and the global community as a whole are seemingly perplexed, wondering what to do next about the resolution of challenging and declining marriages, and now a sexless marriage. If a marriage goes, usually there goes the family. When the family's gone; there goes the neighborhood/society. No wonder musical prodigy, Stevie Wonder cried for help from heaven when he song "Heaven Help Us All". Aliens have taken humanity to "Planet Mars." "Somewhere over the rainbow, somewhere far"!

The institution of a marriage will always be the same. It's not going anywhere. God created the institution, which should be highly respected, not dejected, infected, and rejected.

It is the highest form of any institution on earth. Just like any institution, shouldn't you learn the guidelines and bylaws? Why do some research and study those rules and regulations in secular institutions to make it successful and operate smoothly, but neglect to acquire knowledge to have a thriving successful marriage? Let's reflect. Not picking on any particular thing, but let's look at the sports community and its audience. How many seem to be awestruck over football---baseball---basketball---hockey---boxing---golf---skiing---wrestling---car-racing---bowling---rollerblading, etc. The fans at the stadiums and surrounding events seem to know and study every guideline, play, position, strike, etc. Wouldn't it be wonderful if many intensely studied the guidelines for the upkeep of satisfying, pleasing and developing intimate, healthy relationships?

A uniting in matrimony suggests "that two become one", not that two become complete. (Gen. 2:15-18) (Matthew 14:4-5). Your completeness should have been a work in progress before the hook up. The myth that "you become complete" because you got married is just that, a non-truth. What some couples fail to realize is "that the relationship between a husband and a wife should be a 100-100 percent equal proposition, not opposition" suggested by the marriage expert, counselor Dr. Miles Munroe. Could this be the reason why marriages operating on a 50-50 proposition are running rampant like chickens with their head cut off or better yet, a two-headed monster? Understandably, "two half individuals trying to become one, create chaos or much confusion."

Get clarity on the oneness issue as well. Dr. Creflo Dollar, a well-known pastor once quoted the bible, "in all thou getting; get a good understanding." In actuality, when you two discover the true meaning of this concept, you all can become a power team to be reckoned with. Too often couples are disillusioned that they should lose their individuality or identity in the "oneness concept." In too many instances, one partner becomes a "nonperson (in the background of someone else's success)" or "invisible". Psalms 139:14. God made you to be one of a kind. "He" made you an original. Your handprint and fingerprint are different from that of anybody else's---living or dead. Nobody else can do what he assigned you to do! The hip hop mogul, Russell Simmons has a book *"Do You!"* On your journey of discovering what you are created and destined to do, and then do it to the best of your ability. Allow God to do the rest.

Conflicts can arise out of one spouse taking the issue of "oneness" to the extreme. One might take the "authoritative/controlling approach" and think that one can't go anywhere or do anything without the other. He/she makes commanding remarks such as "Don't you step not one foot out of this house without me!" or "Absolutely no visitors until I get back!" and "Quit talking on that telephone while I'm home", etc. When one spouse does not conform to this *concept* according to this "mindset", someone usually rebels and attempts to change the other. The reality is a change has to come from within. As tempting as it might be, you cannot mold a spouse in the concept of a "Step-ford Wife or a Step-ford Husband" (obeying you at your every command). I think not!

Unfortunately, some husbands try to change wives into their mothers. Because some have been under that nurturing environment of having someone cooking, cleaning, washing, and taxing for numerous years, they perceive a wife as the maid service…unless they have been taught differently. Haven't you wondered why they play with the "super freak" (the kind, singer Rick James says "you can't take home to mama, because she's a super freaky" of a woman) but then go scouting for "Ms. Do-Right!" Normally someone similar or close to their mom when it's time to marry!

Yes, mostly everyone yearns for that special bond. The kind of bond, where one spouse got ya back no matter what! Through thick or thin! Go to any links for you. When it's found, it is to be a closer, deeper, more intimate bond like no other. Isn't this why most feel that marriage holds such an extraordinary place? The "Garden of Eden" experience before the fall. These are the couples who will say "My whole complete soul has found my significant other whole complete soul (presumably soul mates)"; "We were destined for each other"; "You make my liver quiver"; No one can fill in the blanks like you baby"; etc. On many occasions they begin to think, act and even feel alike. Are you like the ones who complete each other sentences?

These sound like the couples that are conscious of the belief "that marriage really is ministry and a blood covenant. Marriage is commitment to the institution." No, it's not min-is-try (I'll try it and if I don't like it, then I'll see you later)! Through some trials and errors, some bumps and lumps along the way, they acquired knowledge, balance, wisdom and discipline and they finally figured out that marriage really was not to be entered into lightly. It should go beyond the: ~cake ~date ~lake ~limousine ~cuisine ~flowers ~wedding showers ~gowns and the presents. This would include a "*shared*" involvement of prayer, household duties, and quality time together, giving of them-selves, communicating and listening to each other, upholding and protecting the commitment of their vows, etc.

In the natural, marrying someone can be risky, but isn't life? Marriage can be love and it can be pain, but remember that God will be that shelter from the strain that marriage sometimes bring. When negative situation begin to happen in your marriage, don't throw in the towel, howl if you must. You might even ask yourself the question. "Why Did I Get Married?" Some of us could relate to that movie produced by the *"Renaissance Man"*, Mr. Tyler Perry. Did we marry for love, lust or security as some of the couples did in the movie?

The Bible teaches "that the marriage itself is honorable" (Hebrews 13:4) but *beware*, that the individuals united might not necessarily be so. Be real. We all have flaws in our paws and jaws. This is especially true of individuals who were not joined by the hip, but by their lips. *This is considered being married by man in the flesh by lust.* Dr. Robin L. Smith, author of *"Lies at the Altar"* explains in her book that "those waves of passion and ecstasy coursing through our bodies are the product of a pronounced spike in *dopamine, a hormone* that produces feelings of pleasure, and *nor epinephrine, which is similar to adrenaline and increases excitement.*"

Wow! "This combination of these chemicals perhaps cause that exquisite lovesickness that some experience in the early stages of love", according to Dr. Smith's book. Is this the kind that makes some go SOS {Stuck-On-Stupid or as the old folks say "smelling yourself"}…and no one can tell you anything or your head becomes hard and you don't listen? Everybody else seems to be wrong. Y'all against the world! There are songs out there to fit you all and urge you on the more. Nope, don't blame it on the rain…blame it on the love potion chemicals, lol. Not only is the drug fast-acting, it leaves your system quickly, according to some experts. They have to come out of a false illusion of that "puppy love" (teenage love). Leave "Fantasy" Island and revisit planet Earth. In sum, this should be the point where your marriage begins the phases of progression after the honeymoon is over. This will decide how grownup you can be. What separates the men from the boys or the women from the girls? The mature from the immature!

Sure, there should be a difference in marriages that God joined together and those that he didn't have anything to do with. This is found in Matthew 19:4-6: What therefore *God hath joined together* let no man put asunder. How could this be? According to Dr. Munroe, "two individuals that are operating by spiritual laws, rules or principles that are maintaining a consistent balance that increase productivity; peace; joy; an overall satisfaction with life and longevity in the relationship" sounds like marriages of the God-kind.

The trailblazing actor, Will Smith directed and starred in an award winning movie "The Pursuit of Happiness." If spouses fail to stay continuously in "hot pursuit" for creating an environment for a thriving marriage, then don't be tripping that your matrimony isn't dripping with the roses, carousel, and caramel with cherries and whip cream on top. Not saying that they have a perfect union, but in the realm of spiritual values, international spiritual leader, Dr. Frederick Price says, "they should deal honestly with those spiritual aspects first, so that the rest of the challenges might fall into place and both persons will not make haste to end the relationship without doing everything to make it successful". They realize that they can agree to disagree.

Many non-Christians and Christians went to a Church; some went to the Justice of the Peace, and others they just went. They went through a ceremony and through some rituals. Not fully understanding that being married in a church building or any other facility does not mean God has put that husband and wife together. Get equally yoked and not choked. If you're not alert, some will even smoke and roast ya; tie you up and fry ya!

Based on God's kingdom principles, the marital order has placed the husband as the head of the household---certainly not the *task master* of the household to rule with a rod. Does it possibly hold true that many husbands use Ephesians 5:22-24 and take that scripture out of context to dominate or control the wife? Surveys and research has shown over the years "that there's an absence of men in some churches and presumably they have abdicated their leadership. Therefore, women have taken on the role as headship (at least in practice if not in name)." When husbands take their rightful role as being the lover, provider, protector and respecter of his wife and family, just as Jesus was the Lover, Provider, and Protector of the Church, couples experiencing heavenly marriages on earthly territory *shall be the rule rather than the exception.* If husbands truly want to know how to behave toward their wives and not treat them like pet slaves; study the love manual…the Bible.

Have you ever heard of Jesus being abusive toward the Church? Husbands, God won't even hear your prayers if you don't treat your wife right. Read (1st Peter 3:7), (Ephesians 5:25-33) and examine the consequences of treating your wife unfairly. The mistreatment of your wife will result in opening an unwanted door of sickness, disease, poverty, and sometimes premature death.

For the wives that strive to boss at any cost, are you ready to face the loss of covenant blessings? The word "*submit*" is legit in Ephesians 5:22, 1st Peter 3:1-6. Just go ahead, it kinda makes you wanna say "ouch" without a doubt. The fall of Adam and Eve getting hauled out of the "Garden of Eden" due to disobeying God resulted as punishment for the woman to become subservient. Is this why author, Pastor John Hagee stated in his book "What every Man Wants In a Woman," that "only a Spirit-filled woman can submit to a God-fearing man that respects his wife?" Can this be categorized as a "godly submission?" This is not to say that, "a morally good woman cannot!" What about a "worldly submission" to abuse that leads to bondage---therefore women and men suffer unjustly? Ex: "He/she doesn't mean to hurt me; besides, a little smacking once in a while won't kill me." "It felt strange to not hear my man/woman cussing and fussing, where's the love," some will comment. *Too often, the beating or verbal mistreatment is confused with love.*

Ephesians 5:21, should bring many back from cardiac arrest and set you at ease after Paul saying this: "...**submitting yourselves one to another in the fear of God**." Does this suggest that neither is subordinate nor controlling and that through Christ, equality has set you back in your right position? This equality means that you all are on equal terms as *respecting, loving, and sharing*; nevertheless, the scripture states that "the man is still the head of his household."

Please note that after reviewing the definition of marriage

by several marital experts, in summation, they suggest that "**marriage** is much more than a contractual legal agreement to sleep together physically and share the obligations of the family finances. Marriage is the combination of two souls connecting and coming into unity in which lies the *center of submission (to each other)*, conviction and values, moral and spiritual insight." Yet marriage is not for everybody and neither is living alone. Undeniably, two are better than one. Aren't you glad to know that marriage is not a requirement to serve God or go to heaven? It's certainly not a necessity to be successful in life. Phew! Waiting to exhale! Now go ahead.

Another important part of the ministry in a marriage is sex. Yes, believe it or not. It is not just for producing children (procreation). It's also for enjoyment and pleasure. After all, isn't it about intimacy? Intimacy comes in different forms such as: small gestures as holding hands while strolling in the park, back rubbing, foot massages, phone calls, text messages, e-mails or a date at the movies. Back to the basics of kissing or smooching and hugging! Dr. Phil eloquently suggests that "*sex* is not the foundation of a healthy relationship, it is a natural extension of a relationship in which giving and receiving natural support and comfort is common."

Legal sex is supposed to be safe and pleasurable with a marriage license. According to 1st Corinthians 7:3..."Let the husband render to his wife the affection due her." In the King James Version it also reads "render unto the wife due benevolence." There used to be a saying "ain't nothing due but the rent." That phrase can be extended as to "ain't nothing due but the rent or the mortgage, the car note, or the bills...so why not sex when ya enter matrimony?"

The author Gary Chapman of "*The Four Seasons of Marriage*" states that, "over a course of a marriage some couples will experience a significant change in their sexual relations. Other conflicts over sexual boredom, sexual hang-ups and restrictions arise if they are not willing to grow and adapt to differences in each other's sexual preferences." Will you both be willing to stretch yourselves sexually (sometimes different positions *that you are both comfortable with*) rather than sticking with the same pattern of things that you all like in common?

Are you like some of us who have gotten the "miseducation concept" of sex being love. Careful research and examination has shown the relationship counselor and expert, Dr. Miles Munroe that "sex is 100 percent physical and chemical. The trouble began when we equate love with sex. Sex is a physical coupling of two people---a joining of flesh-to-flesh.

True love is a spiritual uniting between two people---a joining of spirit to spirit." According to the world's eyesight, "love and sex are synonymous." Isn't it plastered in magazines; books; movies; videos; TV programs, etc?

On the other hand, for some wives, it can be no big deal. As long as their partner is expressing affection by touching, caressing, and romancing. For a lot of husbands, taking it away usually have him in disarray and dismayed. The only time that it's biblically scriptural for husbands and wives to deprive each other of sexual activities with consent for a time, so that they may give themselves to fasting and prayer; and then they are to come together again so that the adversary does not tempt them because of their lack of control, 1st Corinthians 7:5. Wisdom will tell you also to refrain if one or the other spouse is ill. The final decision is between you and God or common sense tells you to withhold the sex because of a continuously betrayal of a cheating spouse who says he/she want or can't quit, (his/her actions are speaking louder than words) regardless of all the marital counseling sessions, and ultimatums given. Warning: unless God's grace and mercy is shielding you from some incurable and life threatening diseases, you will experience the unpleasant affects that they can bring.

In Chapter Nine of *"The Separated"*, some discovered

that the split will un-knit your bond further physically. Others could finally see when they were set free.

CHAPTER NINE

THE SEPARATED

Perhaps a separation might end the commitment, but couples still experience emotional attachments. Most couples experiencing this usually find themselves "in-and-out" of the relationship. Remember the song, *"It's So Hard to Say Good Bye to Yesterday"*!....Boyz II Men. Friends and acquaintances are puzzled as to whether or not if they are truly separated. One minute they are intending on getting back together, then the next minute they're un-mending. They're up and down a roller coaster deciding where to get off this bumpy saga and saying, "Are we there yet" for a stable, peaceful landing to this episode? Isn't it ironic, they barely get along and don't want to see each other when they are together? The moment they separate, some act like playmates on a date.

Many confess that "if they had not parted ways from the chaos of the relationship, they would have continued restless days on the edge of stepping off a ledge." Insanity would have been their plight and humanity would have put them out of sight in the mental institution. Some dearly departed argue their point by saying "Absence makes the heart grow fonder"…but it could make his heart and wallet a lot more forgetful about you. "Out of sight, out of mind!" In some instances, absence does work. Woe, if you let 'em roam too long though, they'll be gone. They'll be gone emotionally, physically, and before ya know it financially. A sista gone say, "Now you can take my honey but don't take away my money, but I ain't no gold digger."

The other dearly departed assumed that a separation will bring clarity. They will either have a resolve or a dissolve. According to the experts this will give them time to reevaluate their relationship, and for some their priorities. Some allow themselves the time to think or reflect. Others might want to sink into a hole and grow old instead of confronting the issue at hand. According to Robert S. Weiss's book *Marital Separation*, "most separations; however, are neither peaceable nor anticipated. Partners can become unlinked *permanently*." A golden nugget: Each state can vary regarding a legal or formal separation. It addresses issues regarding the custody of the children, house, child support, and alimony, etc. Check the status of the time limit that allows you to remain separable.

For the ones who just haul and go A-WOL and walkout without the ails of a paper trail. Ya know how some do when they don't want the hoopla. They can go on and on singing to that Oscar performance heartfelt song "*No More Drama*" by the soulful Ms. Mary J. Blige. Try not to moan and groan too long. The "abandonment" process can leave you without anything. It might be a little rough in getting your stuff that you're entitled to. "Can you feel it, can you feel it, hey hey hey, good-bye!"

In actuality, sometimes one spouse or the other is trying to prolong the inevitable of divorce…if it were ever considered; so they separate indefinitely. However, some fall into infidelity [and for some a second or third time, etc.] They have come to terms with the fact that they are not going to patch things up. The kinks that were once molehills are now mountains. This is pushing their relationship on the brink of moral decay.

"*The Divorced*" in Chapter Ten was forced to get off the merry-go-round and face the music. They no longer want to pretend that everything is fine.

CHAPTER TEN

THE DIVORCED

Now, how did I get to this point, you might be asking? "What happened?" "What went wrong?" "How could she/he expect me to be a saint if I can't have the cookie/nookie?" "Surely she/he didn't base our marriage on sex alone, wasn't our love supposedly to have been enough to sustain us?" "I thought we were inseparable!" "Somehow the absence made us grow further apart" "I give up, I'm tired of working on this marriage", etc. These are just some of the phrases these couples are left pondering over after this devastating event that has happened in their lives.

The truth of the matter is many couples were not properly equipped or informed and did not know what it took to create and sustain a satisfying, committed and healthy relationship. If you were like most, by the time you acquired the necessary information, you were too tired or it took too much energy to put into action. Usually when the husband/wife wakes up and realizes that he/she wants to change and get help, suddenly the husband/wife wants a divorce. In some instances, the other partner grows cold, become bitter, and develops a negative attitude. As the feisty, legendary Ms. Patti Labelle sings in her uplifting song...*A New Attitude.* And those who did not enter marriage blindly and thought they had known what they were getting into are traumatized. Don't be too hard on yourselves.

Many unexpected pop-ups or temptations arose that you could not have possibly foreseen down the road. You both brought a lot of emotional, psychological and other baggage of experiences, memories and habits. Invisible Skeletons are in both of your past that you were not honest enough to reveal. The dynamic Ms. Roberta Flack's "Killing Me Softly" caught you off guard and that song, *with his/her negative words,* became your national anthem. Therefore, unknowingly those words cut through the core of one's spirit and brought about resentment and hatred. This is why so many surprisingly air everything out on *"Divorce Court"* with Judge Lynn Toler, Dr. Phil Show, Judge Judy, Jerry Springer, Good Morning America, The National Enquirer or The Legendary Oprah Winfrey Show. The burdens of keeping secrets were just unbearable. Some just like to blab it all...blabber mouths. Others just love the drama!

Naturally, many people do change during the course of their marriage. You have some changing for the better, and others for the worse. Remember big breasted, double D wife Jill that you knew have had a sex change. Her new name is now Bill. After Will swallowed the hormonal pill, "he" became "she". The "*Dr. Jekyll/Ms. Hyde*" inevitably showed up! Maybe some of you can identify with this schizophrenia pattern listed here: "You just be you", she says; "but once we're hitched, "*Sophia's* home and thangs are changing around here (Color Purple)"! *She snapped and did a one hundred and ninety degree turnaround.* "Yes, I have forgiven you for your cheating...the bedroom door is always opened unless you stop bringing that money home, lol. Quickly the headaches' emerges on many occasions"!!! What used to be debates have turned into disrespectful arguments, and some with physical altercations along with emotional and mental abuse.

So many couples had come to the conclusion that they were not going to masquerade a false front any more. Because life really is too short, why waste valuable time? Why deny my happiness? We're already emotionally detached and sexually starved from the relationship anyway. So they started acting out a single lifestyle. Many were acting as if they were not committed to a spouse anymore. Especially bickering over the same arguments, major or minor; which they knew that it should have been resolved before the marriage had gotten to such a detrimental state. It makes you wonder "Can a leopard change its spots?" Most of these arguments that dealt with communication, infidelity, money, religion, honesty, children and sex [or lack of] to name a few; continuously led to the unhappiness.

What's that saying, "If Mama Ain't Happy, Ain't Nobody Happy?" Not even the dog lol! Rather than using the gun after conflicts, some took the plunge toward the inevitable. Many were hesitant to go the divorce route because it once was of the belief that "a lot of couples, especially Christians, would remain in marriages miserable because some Church and their members and our culture treated them like second, third or fourth class citizens and made them feel like failures if they were divorcees". People claiming to know and love Jesus treated "them" like some people that are not saved, cold and cruel. Does this "concept" hold true today?

You have many walking around in a state of depression for years. They felt like this was the ultimate failure. What it all boils down to are feelings of rejection or insecurity, says the experts. Then, if they are not careful; they will become very vulnerable---followed by low self esteem. Anyone who gives them attention...a rendition of what they desire to hear, they will be at "the altar" again or back in the sheets with "Mr. Big or Ms. Smith" before they were healed from the previous marriage/relationship. *"Oops I Did It Again"* a song by the talented Britney Spears; the song becomes their mantra. How about the infamous country singer Willie Nelson's hit *"On the Road Again"*...I've got to get on that marital road again? It's really time for someone to consider counseling! Whether that's alone sessions, group therapy, and there's online therapy. Don't be ashamed! It could be your gain.

Just because divorce is *running rampantly* in society today does not mean that you have to become a statistic. Then, if you are, *this does not mean the death of you as an individual or that your life is over.* Although divorce was not God's perfect design for man and woman, and "He" hates divorce; "He" also does not want you hurting. Yes, marriage is sacred and you believed that giving up on your marriage was not an option. Assuredly divorce can be very, very, devastating and traumatic, and it can take a toll on you emotionally, physically, and financially. Will you forever allow people to put you into bondage if you are already divorced or thinking about it? Who can assure you as to how often one can bounce back from a life-threatening situation and life full of unnecessary suffering? Didn't Jesus Christ die for this? Cast all your cares on Jesus. He'll be that rock that you can lean and depend on.

Will we dare stare into the eyes of another angry, hurting

generation, watch their demise, and nonchalantly ask in Chapter 11 *"What About the Children"*?

CHAPTER ELEVEN

WHAT ABOUT THE CHILDREN?

Yes, it could be safe to say that they will be alright when they are young and unaware of this sexless lifestyle arrangement. What happens when they grow up and observe, and imitate parents' lifestyles? The example that was modeled that it's okay for parents to lead separate and sexless lives! As we all know, some children pattern their parents very well, whether we like it or not. Should this be the legacy, which parents would leave their children, married with a sexless lifestyle?

Sadly, too many parents are unaware of the terminator's [devil] devices of desiring their children to be terminated emotionally and physically. He does this by having some of them aborted daily before entering this world. After this fails, he attacks their innocence, creative spirit by stirring confusion in their dysfunctional home environment through fights, neglect, incest, molestation, abuse, rejection and abandonment. In childhood, all criticisms, rejection, and blame are usually taken personally. Therefore, the residue of toxic relationships can resurface in their adolescence. In addition, there are some children that live in surroundings that are not healthy; they view this lifestyle as normal. Girls running into the arms of men for a sense of belonging...young or old (many of them experiencing and accepting abuse on every level), because they were looking for fatherly attention and love in all the wrong faces and places! Women lay in prey on young boys to toy and experiment with them and who are undoubtedly exploiting them as well.

Is this why some children act out in bad behavior that grownups find inexcusable and unacceptable; yet, they have created this? Some repeat this mirrored cycle. King of Pop, Michael Jackson's *"Man in the Mirror"* song sounds as if it has merit to it. Those words in the song challenges one (adults) to look in the mirror and make that change. [Children normally do as we do and not always do as we say]. Most children can adapt to any environment, surroundings or lifestyles with no problems. These are the ones who purposely try to avoid being like the negative parent/s or environment and choose to be a better person despite their obstacles. Then, there are the other children who become insecure, rebellious, confused, traumatized, and vulnerable and repeat the unhealthy cycle they have lived.

During the adolescent years, quite a few become curious or questionable as to why their parents are in separate bedrooms or living in separate rooms of the house. Their inquisitiveness eventually puts two and two together. They begin to observe the pattern of one parent being absence from the house all night/days/weeks/months. They presume if ain't no satisfaction in the bedroom at home; it possibly could be going on elsewhere. Not necessarily always the case!

Naturally, children want parents to be together, but it is not always possible. When the foundation of a home is shaken by betrayal due to infidelity or other circumstances, the home environment often becomes challenging or sometimes deteriorate. Because the adolescent and young adult years are one in which they recognize the tension and frustration and seems to be impacted by it the most; is being cordial, respectful and peaceable too much of a resolution to ask for the sake of the children? Witnessing many conflicts, drama, heated discussions or whatever you choose to call it, you should not be surprised at the overwhelmingly response of youth that does not want any part of a marital institution. They would rather tip and dip and shack! Especially if this is all that they have to look forward to, a dysfunctional marriage…and now one without sex! Shouldn't one generation be better than the previous one? Isn't it time that somebody break this cycle?

Chapter Twelve *"Danger Zone: No Sex In Marriage"* Are you safe or are you on the chase for another…about to lose your significant other because the love tank is about to sank into oblivion?

CHAPTER TWELVE

DANGER ZONE: NO-SEX IN MARRIAGE

There are couples who, for a variety of reasons are sexless. Many factors lead up to no sex in the marriage. Whether it was due to biological challenges, personal and emotional challenges, cultural challenges, or relational challenges, *Infidelity* ranked very high as one of the chief contributing factor. For many of the potential causes of this dilemma have been identified, some couples need to be aware of the affects that no loving libido might have on their relationship. What are they going to do about it?

Ah, some of these wives are saying: "Why are we always the ones who have to be doing something about it?" "Why is everybody always picking on us and expecting us to do right?" "We're not the fix it women." "What about our husbands?" "It's their fault that we are in this predicament anyway." "Does it always have to be about their egos?" "Husbands"! "They need to just grow up and do right." "Practice self-control!" "We can, why can't they?" Men on the other hand are saying, "Why doesn't she give it up and do her marital duties?" "If she doesn't, someone else will!" "Doesn't she know that women are a dime a dozen?" "Did she forget that we men need sex like women need to talk?" All of these comments are well founded, but they are not going to change a thang. It's time to smell the coffee, not the coffin---wishful thinking will not change things, prayer, meditating, communications and actions do.

Remember wives, the assumption that you are going to withhold the cootie, bootie as a form of punishment for his betrayal might be alright for a while; when it becomes a lifestyle, it is a different story altogether....especially if he has reformed from a cheating lifestyle. You were doing this for temporary punishment until you could figure out some type of solution for your pain and anger. *Naturally*, you should be allowed to go through your stages of withdrawal, or grieving process. Until they have walked in the shoes of infidelity, they can't fathom the emotions. If you have, your response can differ from theirs. Golden nugget: *don't react out of your emotions and don't play the victim role forever*! Rekindling the sexual flame again will entail a lot of challenging moments. Prep and take baby steps! *Time heals! This too shall pass*! One day your **mess** will **bless** and become a message of prevention, hope and healing to someone. Your **test** will be a **testimony**! Realistically, we know that a lot of men are not going to hold out, they'll pout and scout

out who's available.

"In actuality, some husbands intensely need loving on a sexual level and reassurance of their male functioning skills" according to some studies. Being denied sex over a length of time only makes them more vulnerable to becoming bait to vulnerable females as well. With the widespread of pornography via internet, television, illicit media of sexual advertising all around, some will look for love/lust or sex in any venue. What happens when your husband is approached by: Ms. Tramp, Vamp, Traitor, Snitch of a Witch, and *itch of a woman and he falls prey? He'll be singing the blues and to the tune of the "just can't help it". You will be screaming Mr. Ray Charles song, *"What kind a Man Are You?"*

To those husbands that is keeping slick "Willie" on lockdown to punish your mate when things are not great, "Bo-dilly" is around the corner waiting on yo' "Ms. Chilly". One's refusal to get medical attention or help for your low sexual desire will retire her from your arms…into the charm of another. Visiting a doctor early could offset unnecessary future problems. Urologists are specialist for diagnosing testosterone levels.

Some experts suggest "that the result of no-sex in a marriage will lead to a miscarriage of pleasurable fulfillment, sleeplessness, and released tension which sex was intended to do." Yes, even medical doctors, psychologists and researchers have discovered "that active sexual relations can take years off of your life and keep you looking youthful." The famous Dr. Oz of *"The Oprah Winfrey Show"* says that your physiological age can be reduced by six years if you have more than 200 orgasms." Duke University did this study that surveyed people on the amount and quality of sex they had. Are you aware that "being sexual with a beloved partner has proven benefits for your health", according to Dennis Surgue, Ph.D, Clinical Associate Professor of Psychiatry of the University of Michigan Medical School and past president of the American Association of Sex Educator, Counselor and Therapists? These include "the health benefits of touch, lowered high blood pressure and cholesterol, increased blood flow to the rest of your body that would reduce stress, boosting your immune system and even helping you cope with pain." Because anti-inflammatory chemicals are produced in the body and pain-killing chemicals are released in the brain during sex, could the absence of sex deprive you of that *"Sexual Healing"* expressed in this song by the late musical prodigy "Mr. Marvin Gaye"? Dr. Oz also suggest "that when you connect with another person on a physically intimate level, and particular when you reach orgasm [zen experience], you generate a cascade of biochemical reactions that cause you to fly high as an eagle."

Also, included is "the healing power of the spiritual and emotional aspect of intimacy (and the ability of sharing this sexual act to knit/bond you to your spouse").

Especially true of some men says the Berman sisters [Dr. Jennifer Berman, director of the Female Sexual Medicine Center at UCLA Medical Center in Los Angeles and Dr. Laura Berman, director of the Berman Center and a professor of ob-gyn and psychiatry at Northwestern University in Chicago] "sex is not only about a sexual release: but a closeness to a spouse; sense of validation or attractiveness; sense of importance; and achieving an emotional intimacy." They want to be appreciated or needed…that {hero syndrome}. Sex for some women means "the Midas touch." For some, their men don't have to put out often as long as they experience the touch of patting on their body, pecking or necking, cuddling or hugging {non-sexual intimacy} often gives them that feeling that they are special and she's the number one girl who rocks his world.

Just the warmth of him around…doing chores together brings a pleasurable intimate bonding. Moreover, if this leads to being romantically inspired to something else, then so be it. The lack of this experience can sometimes result in rejection, alienation, anger, pain, hurt, sadness and frustration. Additionally, it could result in discouragement, defensiveness, contempt, non-communication, and an emptiness that will leave one or both partners vulnerable. These kinds of emotions will open the door for all kinds of temptation! Couples began to struggle with their self-esteem. The blinders are taken off.

The vulnerable, faithful wife starts creeping. "Who's making love to your old lady/man while you were out making love?" Could this possibly be a true saying? She not only cheats with a man, she begins testing the water with women. Something she swore she would never do. "Never say never!" Some experts suggest that "a woman's emotions and sexuality are closely connected and that's why she becomes affected so strongly. If she's not careful, she will become deceived by the emotional fulfillment that she gets from another female as sexual love." She's struggling with being heterosexual, bi-curious, or bisexual.

The frustrated husband usually can separate his sexuality from his emotions. It is mostly stated that, "he thinks with what is between his legs and fall in bed, bump his head with males and females solely as experimentations with no serious attachments." What happens when these unnatural affections clutch and hook him? *Beware*! When you start testing the waters with the same sex, they say "it's a challenging spirit to break." What's that phrase: "Once you smoke crack, it's hard to get back to your senses." (Nothing is impossible with God). That kind only comes out by continuous fasting and prayer. So is the spirit of homosexuality.

This kind of disorder does not flow with the foundation of God's roadmap…the Bible. God does not hate the lesbian or the homosexual. The lesbian and homosexual lifestyle does not fit into God's command: "to be *fruitful* and multiply." This is the Gospel truth according to Genesis 1:28. Has there ever been a report of same sex physically, sexually connecting and getting pregnant and conceiving?

The emotions of (resentment, anger, and bitterness) that you might have felt you deserved to feel and express toward your spouse/partner after infidelity has reversed themselves toward you. They act as if you are the cause of their shortcomings. You're saying, "Don't he/she have some nerves." *Now*, insult is added to injury. Seeds of animosity, revenge, and vindictiveness are grappling many couples' mind. The battle between the sexes is brewing.

The husband/wife believes they are justified to cheat even the more without remorse, because of your refusal…especially if they have felt that they have turned from their cheating ways, and he/she's showing accountability of his/her whereabouts and displaying a role of faithfulness &

commitment. Is this why, it is of the belief "that when one put a halt on the sex; quite a few become a wreck and some become addicted to pornography? Others become addicted to something else that is usually not beneficial. The indulgence of alcohol to numb the pain of being in a sexless marriage has emerged. What little chance of the marriage becoming salvageable has been placed further on the back burner," according to articles by *"Hopeful Solutions for Your Sexless Marriage"*! Because of ongoing liaisons, eventually your spouse see you and your secret lover together, both of y'all could wind up on the six and ten o'clock news. Who knows, it could become prime time.

When you are in a sexual drought, might one develop unemotional connectedness, lack of enthusiasm for the marriage, depression, withdrawn, overeating or not eating, insecurity emotional and mental stress, unusually critical of each other, feelings of failures, loss of femininity and masculinity, and frustration, etc? Now, the best kept secret in a book *"The Sex-Starved Wife"* by Michele Weiner Davis about men "low sexual desire" that's turning wives into beehives. Buzzing and fussing relentlessly about her unfulfilled, chill of a lacking sex life. "I have occasionally hopped on top to make it pop to get an erection! After many attempts, he won't bulge. He simply nudges me out the door. Leaving me sobbing on the floor", says some wives! Sadly, because of the embarrassment, shame, frustration, guilt, pride and a sense of failure, some men will not talk nor get help by going to visit a doctor or get therapy and possibly a sexologist for this minor interruption. As a result, marriages are suffering. "At times this treatment can move a sexless marriage to a marriage that ends in a separation (emotionally or physically) or a legal divorce" according to some experts.

No doubt, many are not "*Counting the Cost*" as specified in Chapter Thirteen. They have seen "the good, the bad and the ugly." Some get lost in it all and toss everything. Others just glean and come clean.

CHAPTER THIRTEEN

COUNTING THE COSTS

You often hear remarks about "how bad of a shape this world is in". Or "if people don't start taking better care of the planet and its environment, our children will not have a safe or healthy place to dwell." "A Planet in Peril"! "I hope that someday things will improve." "It's got to, or we are all doomed!" Yeah, sure you're right! Mostly everyone is somewhat aware of the chaotic state due to the media's documentaries about the planet's crisis, which is termed "global warming."

Could the same hold true about the crisis of marriages? Now can you believe a sexless one? Society as a whole would say: "An estimated twenty percent of marriages of the sexless kind have got to be unrealistic. You've got to be kidding me!", "It seems like every month or so there's a cheating scandal flashing across the TV or in the headlines...how alarming?" "So many marriages are in trouble", "Isn't it sad about the appallingly high fifty percent divorce rate"?, "Some of the other half that remains are mostly enduring with little satisfaction and living in despair", "Couples are not as committed as they used to be", "I hope that they can get it together and things will change", etc. The ones who are actually trying to do what they can to stop the decline concerning the crisis are overwhelmed and frustrated. The others will not let it deter them from pushing forward in hopes of change and doing the best they can. With so many distractions, schedules, appointments, engagements, one can only speculate if anyone is really tending to their relationship. Like so many, they got caught up in the "show and tell" of having "the wedding"; and never prepared for matrimony. Quite a few did not want the run of a mill wedding, so they went over the hill in debt and now they fret about any and everything. Can you imagine some are still holding on to unforgiveness about the past debt?

Marriage can be likening unto a computer. It constantly needs upgrading or an overhaul. Supposedly operating just the way it should at optimum performance level. However; a year/years later, after much use, wear and tear, or downloading lots of programs, this usually pose a conflict with its operating system. Often times a virus can infiltrate your computer. With this virus, unexpected unwanted pop-ups come on your screen and interrupt whatever you're working on. And we all know that this can become very annoying, unless you have a good tolerance level. Although you press the exit button and they disappear temporarily, you have not fixed the problem. The longer the virus spreads, the more it affects your computer and the more annoying pop-ups you encounter. Because of delayed or non-repair, your privacy becomes threatened and you could lose all of your valuable data and information that were stored. The sooner you repair them, the less expense. The longer you prolong or procrastinate and wait, the costlier it becomes.

Some couples or relationships might not require a level of care on a daily basis. They have installed their anti-virus preventive measure software (love-communication enablers or enhancements) to keep the flame/spark running efficiently. However, your relationships will sometime encounter unexpected pop-ups that are beyond your ability to predict or control. Pop-ups such as:

> Financial issues
> Family issues
> Sickness
> Disease
> Hardships
> Aging
> Adultery
> Loss of a job

> ➢ Loss of a loved one

and other challenges are inevitable. The iconic *Queen of Talk Show* host Oprah Winfrey has an infamous quote, "What I Know for Sure." What I know for sure about *life and circumstances* is that "*it will change*". When the storms of life come, no one is immune. One of America's most influential; spiritual leader and well-known author, Pastor T. D. Jakes of the Bestseller "*Repositioning Yourself*", suggests that "people must position and reposition themselves" when it does.

Usually all of us are constantly facing changes. This does not mean that we all receive and respect the change. For some according to Dr. Leonard N. Smith in a May/June 2007 magazine called "*Gospel Today*" [pastor of the Mt. Zion Church in Arlington, Va. And president of Richmond Virginia Seminary in Richmond, VA] the change "may deliver pain, panic, paranoia, anger, and depression, for others, it can deliver promises, probabilities, possibilities, acceptance, resolutions or constructive actions. A change can be a welcomed visitor or an uninvited intruder! It is strictly up to the individual." The single's counselor and author, "Michelle Hammond" gives us another perspective on change. "The concept of **needful change** is often overlooked. A change, however, could be looked at as *growth*." How you *respond* to the changes or an overload of these pop-ups can determine your productiveness and effectiveness or ineffectiveness. Negative responses can result in aging or stress and can cause a breakdown in your immune system. Gospel extraordinaire song "*A Change*" has come o- o- over me hits home with a lot of folks when they obviously are not responding negatively when drama confronts and flesh wants to rise up.

Umn-hm! Things left unattended or unmanaged usually don't survive. Especially on their own! What use is hoping that your sexless marriage will get back on track if you don't put any action or effort behind it to help you to at least try and resolve the issue that's preventing you from connecting sexually? If you don't do the work, you certainly won't reap the benefits. You might say "that I don't know how or where to begin or have the necessary skills." "People perish for lack of knowledge…Hosea 4:6"! The internet is a very great start. Then, there's the bookstore or library, articles, workshops, conferences and seminars with self-improvement materials. Now some shows such as Dr. Phil, Dr. Laura Berman, OWN (Oprah Winfrey Network), Tyler Perry's new show "*For Better or Worse*" and others are now addressing these issues. The primary responsibility of making this kind of relationship functioning will require the involvement of two human beings who are willing to *admit* and *owning* your share of responsibility to the dysfunction of this union.

Marrying individuals whose careers are demanding and ones that often keep them apart intimately, physically, and emotionally should discuss these situations. These distant and demanding careers/relationships can sometimes create greater strains and friction in an already challenging relationship. *"Strangers in The Night,"* song by legendary Mr. Frank Sinatra sometimes becomes evidence of how a distant relationship progresses. Undeniably, their sex life is put on hold.

Usually, if some couples do not come to a negotiation: "Let the boxing match begin." "Even if the decision to be sexless is thoroughly explained and one might understand to a certain degree, that person's response still might result in confusion first and then resentment", according to some experts. The majority of the time it does not matter if it's "their" fault about them committing adultery; the average man still demands sex, whether you like it or not. Or your highly-sex natured wife becomes agitated by your constant pulling away from her sex advances, begins to contemplate straying. Research has shown that "hurtful feelings will evolve and they will question the love that you all have between each other. The wife giving in to the pressure of having sex when she is not feeling like it or marital rape can result in bitter resentment." What use to be rendezvous at *Paradise Retreat* has now become many sleepless nights at *"Heartbreak Hotel."*

It becomes unfortunate that some of them cannot afford to change their careers due to their overwhelming financial status. The on-rising cost of living and the effect of the media's portrayal of our worsened economy, many that are working minimum wage jobs can barely survive on their income. Because of society pressure or whatever (many fear of not keeping up with the Joneses materialistically) is disheartening. They attest to the comment "that it's hell without money." Their mismanagement of finances or the lack of it what is necessary to keep their lifestyles functioning is too surreal. Many suggest "that finances could possibly run neck to neck with infidelity as the causes of many dysfunctional and failed marriages."

Although our culture has conditioned or trained some women to be the care-givers/takers of the relationship; does this mean that they have to tolerate everything (especially if it's not in God's order)? *"It Takes Two Baby"*...unforgettable duo "Sonny and Cher"! Women take on too much guilt and shame. "If anything goes wrong, they didn't work hard enough to make it right", they say to themselves. Studies reveal "that some men are trained to be Me-focused and women are trained to be Other-focused." Personal happiness seems to have taken precedent over the unity of the family.

Decide if this type of mentality is benefitting you. Get God-focused. Does it make some of you fight the good fight too long and keep you in situations that are not productive for you and can become harmful to your long-term well-being? Far too long, you will keep pondering the same old issues. You'll find yourself like the children of Israel, circling those same mountains/issues over and over again.

Because some women have taken the brunt of disrespect for so long, they have decided to flip the script. The liberated wives are becoming frustrated, angry and opinionated. They are evolving and demanding more. They expect men to be equally domestic around the house as well, etc. Naturally so, some wives/women are working two and three jobs and expected to come home and work! Some of the husbands/men working one job sits on the couch flipping channels or on the computer corresponding with a mistress/s and expects dinner. Sadly, some wives/females become "scorned" women out for the kill of anything regarding male species. The need to brutally dog and blatantly disrespect men/boys and their manhood becomes evident. Could this possibly be the reason our jail-houses are full of women/girls?

Are you ready to pull up your boot straps and roll up

your sleeves?   Unless you are willing to go the long haul, become totally committed to the marriage vows through the good, ugly and the bad; how long are you willing to wait? Will you be one of those who never makes a decision to seek help early when the relationship starts to sour and you do nothing? Will you sit "ye" there and die mentally or emotionally and wallow in self pity and waiting around another *five, ten, fifteen* years for circumstances to improve and like so many, life is passing them by?

By this time the marriage is probably sexless and loveless.   Then, you become more bitter, feeble, nearsighted, farsighted or in need of bifocals, hair graying earlier than usual, or not growing at all, tumors on the brain from stress and duress pressure.   Sometimes stress can lead to strokes, heart failure, nervousness, anxiety or panic attack, and a pattern of forgetfulness.   You don't know whether you are going or coming. Walking around in a zombie state! Next, you will be in a mental institution/behavioral facility or you will become addicted or obsessive to something (prescription medicine; alcohol; drugs; gambling; pornography; women/men, etc). Where will the family be then? If you are a young wife, your husband might be off somewhere replacing you with a new younger thang...also they could be off with an older woman...cougar. Your children being so young, they will more than likely have forgotten you. The Bible says each person has his or her own will, and you cannot go against that person's will, nor his thrills or frills and force them to change and see the need to work on the relationship. Some husbands/wives are so set in their ways.

Putting it on the truthful side: If after all the efforts of trying to coerce a spouse to counseling sessions, therapy, doctor, clergy, marriage classes, unending ultimatums and whatever other methods are given and still no change and spouse is content without having sex, (especially a man)---check their motives. If the problem does not consist of a physical handicap, immobility, life threatening and ongoing illnesses, or mutual consent to abstain by both parties, there can be a bigger problem. "There's a dead rat on the line with his behind". I'm not suggesting that there always is...because a lot of men can become too laid back, content and comfortable and will begin to like things just the way they are indefinitely. Most men don't like change, confrontations and very adamant about not visiting a doctor, nor will stop cheating on their own. And never mind a therapist, are you kidding me! Statistics reveal that only about *twenty percent of men with **ED*** (erectile dysfunction) will seek professional help. ED affects over 30 million men in the United States" according to a 1992 National Health and Social Life Survey. Astounding, isn't it? As long as they can continue doing what they desire and are supplied with the free housecleaning and cooking services; it does not matter what you all are not doing together, separate bedrooms, and for some the same bedrooms, etc. Y'all are just coexisting. Are you ready for this lifestyle?

A sexless marriage is no joke! It can poke at the core of one's spirit of existence and you are dealing with so many emotions. ***Depending on whom you ask***...the rejected partner...who spouse refuses to have sex wears a mask and take on the task of dealing with feelings of loneliness, lifelessness, confused and paralyzed, disappointed, drudgery, imprisonment, and a death sentence, yet they try to be happy. The husband that doesn't think no-sex is a problem shows a nonchalant attitude; is very delusional and can work-a-nerve on a sista lol.

The kept wife...the one withholding or refusing to give her spouse sex due to ongoing affairs, she feels like a "secondary virgin." "No more grief and contracting a disease or infections. No, it's not fair; how one dare interrupt your sex life", some might comment. Especially if it was banging! Although it was sacrificed for a ten-minute thrill, she learns to chill with friends or occupy time with other activities. Please note: every person's life is different. Some may remain celibate and really be kept by

God (no sex, no porn or masturbating, no anxiety or frustration and putting energy elsewhere). The others that are not, when they get hot and bothered, they might shop around. This could mean sex toys! lol. On the other hand, they go and play. For those who thought sex was overrated, it is a relief. No more shaking and faking and partaking of many staged performances of fake orgasms. Therefore spending the money without giving up the honey is nice, lol!

There comes a time when you have to "loose that man/woman and let him/her go." I am not suggesting a physical letting go, but a mental one for your health sake. Don't be like so many of those that have said "when you know *that you know* that you know and convinced that they were to leave, and it was from God, you stayed. Yo time was up! Because of F.E.A.R. ("False Evidence Appearing Real"), it held them in captivity and suffering needlessly for years. The fear of not paying bills on their own, unable to afford housing, food, insurance, car payment was so undeniable. How can one deny that God can supply your every need? There are shelters...good and bad, low income housing assistance, job training programs, and support networking groups. Gotta do the research.

Either you're going to shut up or pray up if you choose not to let the terminator [devil] destroy your marriage. Some

Christian folks want you to remember "that your words have power or they can become sour. Watch what you speak concerning your situation." "Death and life are in the power of the tongue" according to Proverbs 18:21. Could you possibly be having what you have been speaking? Ex: "Girl, that no-good husband of man ain't gone never change or do right." "She always nagging about the yard, the trash, will she ever shut up"? You know what, he/she will not as long as you confessing those negative words. Yeah, you might slip up a lot of times and say it's not working. According to some couples, "if you try to get consistent with positive confessions and energy along with prayer mixed with faith, you will begin to see a difference." You might as well try it, because you know you have tried everything else, haven't you? Invest in the *Love Manual* {The Bible}...a book which pertain principles that has universal truths. The author, Stormie O'Martin, successfully adopted this pattern of the latter. Her husband became saved and they have a raving testimony.

ISSUE OF INFIDELITY

Tyrone Davis, "If I Could Turn Back the Hands of Time", they remarked after getting busted/cheating. Some, a one night stand---a fling, rendezvous; or whatever they will label it; the price of passion/lust can cost you everything. Obviously, they forgot about the movie, *"Fatal Attraction"*. The thrill, the excitement, the chase, the conquest, the sneaking around ("Secret Lovers'…the most popular love song in the eighties by duo group *"Atlantic Star"*); in the beginning of most affairs will give you a false illusion of a "Knight in Shining Armor" or "Hero Syndrome". When one partner gets in over his/her head and becomes emotionally attached and desire a deeper commitment than you are able and willing to adhere to, the other party could feel remorseful and wants out. What are you going to do? Are you really prepared for a spark of revenge that could ignite?

"Hell has no fury like a woman scorned!" "A man has no limits to shame when he's been smitten by the lustful flame". An outraged, uncontrollable mistress strikes anything or anyone in her path when she does not want to let go of the relationship and feels jilted and wants to be No. 1. Although some entered the relationship with their eyes opened knowingly that he/she was someone else's husband/wife, he/she was determined to get him/her at any cost. Wives are caught off guard when "the other woman" snaps on her and sometimes going after her children. Wondering what's going on! The innocent wife and children get caught in the middle of all the madness! Some go as far as stalking you.

If this mistress purposely conceives a baby by your

spouse, look out! Brace yourself for "child support drama, visitation drama, communication drama." Many times the finances are taken from the wife and children's household and have to be shared with the mistress. Some of y'all were barely making ends meet in your own household. DRAMA, DRAMA, DRAMA! You'll never have your husband fully. Will you allow him to share his time with the outside family? Could this be the reason some wives are "making the husbands have a procedure that prevent childbearing?" Zip it and clip it! They are no longer sitting passively allowing the drama. Not only are they getting mad, they are getting even by getting lawyers and suing mistresses & husbands. Some are physically fighting too. Every wife is not allowing the other woman's child in her husband's home or dealing with visitation rights. "What's done in the dark; stays in the dark", voices some wives. Or, they are walking out that door and demanding more for their children and themselves. Not putting up with that foolishness. There are love triangles that end in death or near death encounters. Everybody becomes fair game.

Quit murmuring and complaining if you don't have the life you ordered. Order the life what God has purposed for you! Strategize! Get a plan! The ultimate decision is yours. Are you going to remain passive or become aggressive? I don't mean becoming manipulative. "When you dig one ditch, you better dig two." What's that other phrase, "If you can't have what you want, want something else (according to "His" will)?!" "If you don't like what you're getting, then change what you're doing." "If you keep on doing what you're doing, you are going to keep getting what you're getting...*insanity*." "If you do what you've always done; you will get what you have always gotten." We see this clearly in a book titled *"Commanding Your Morning"* by world renowned motivational speaker, life coach teacher Dr. Cindy Trimm. Command a marriage that is healthy and balanced!!!

CONCLUSION

Whether you are a sexless couple that occasionally, infrequently, seldom or have not had sex in years; this book along with some articles have revealed or uncovered that countless others across this nation don't either. However, if they don't deal with this sexless issue, could history repeat itself with yet another generation? It might be alarming and mystifying to some to perceive that some couples do not want to deal with this issue and are settling for this pattern of a lifestyle.

Some of you might be of the rarest if your marital problems do not become clear-cut problems sooner or later. Undeniably, infidelity is becoming a crystal-clear problem that's knocking on so many doors of married and committed couples in this modern era. What about the distinctly heart wrenching problem of spouse abuse (physical; emotional; or mentally) that is becoming commonplace for some? It amazes and becomes mystifying to so many that some of these couples don't find the infrequency of sex; or absence of sex an issue or a problem. Have you ever thought about couples who are not having sex, but the rest of their relationship is just the bomb or hunky dory?

From their standpoint, they have a comfortable and meaningful relationship. "They feel satisfied that their relational needs are met. There is enough love and mutual respect to sustain that relationship," they comment. "A marriage potential for success to them are measured by other factors…like the nature of the problem and level of commitment that is present."

Remembering the old adage "If it ain't broke,..don't fix it?" They are singing their song, "That's Just the Way It Is." "It's all good!" If they are okay with it, then we should be happy glad. They have replaced the action of sex with other expressions of love and are exemplifying a satisfied and successful relationship. Some of these expressions include taking walks on the beach or park; bicycling together; joy riding; visiting museums; trying their hands at cooking or art classes and other thrilling activities; holding hands, fondling, touching, bathing or showering together or intimately connecting, etc.

For those of you in a relationship and would like to deal with your sexless marriage, it can become a long process in figuring out how it got to this point. Truthfully, you probably have forgot, lol! At this stage, it is unimportant if you sincerely desire to fix your marriage, and better yet bringing the sex back. If you are trying to solve the problem you shouldn't have to prove that you're right. Although some of you can recall or reminisce to a time when you did have the flame, made rain, and didn't abstain at the beginning of courtship. Most of you can admit that those early stages may have been the result of lust! Get back to the basics: talking and honestly communicating effectively with an open heart & mind and listening to each other! What happened to well spent time and hanging out? It will take a whole lot of effort and commitment.

According to the marital experts' Bob Berkowitz, PhD and Susan Yager Berkowitz, they suggest that "a sexless marriage is rarely the result of only one partner's behavior, even if it looks that way on the surface." The committed & faithful might beg the difference. Cheating bears no repeating when the two of them are on the same page of set rules of what's agreed upon in the relationship. When one decides to detour from the page of the agreement of rules, set the stage for new rules. Broken rules that violate, more than likely annihilates the agreement. Gwen Stefani song...."No Doubt", it's time to get real and tell your partner the true deal of your desires.

Having a low libido or low sex drive can usually be pinned on either person. According to the infamous relationship expert Dr. Phil, "couples rarely have the same level of sex drive at the same time. Therefore, negotiate for some middle ground that you can both be happy with." "However, if differing levels of desire are causing consistent unhappiness to one or both partner; it is important to resolve it says the experts." Men...how long are you going to allow the shame or embarrassment of not getting an erection or performance anxiety to stop you from visiting a doctor or urologist and maybe a sexologist. Put pride aside and arise to the occasion. Get over it! There are trained certified sex therapist that can teach you many different techniques to overcome these difficulties. Women…you need to snap out of it if you are threatened by a husband's need for pills (such as *Viagra, Cialis, V-Mack* to get an erection. You should be glad he's trying something instead of retreating or withdrawing altogether as so many according to studies.

Golden nugget: stop borrowing other men pills. Get your own prescription from the doctor.

The once able who have become disabled (handicapped) by unforeseen freak accidents, shootings, drunk drivers, or other catastrophes such as war which often entail veterans returning home without the use of limbs or other body parts. They would welcome the opportunity to fill your shoes. Has anyone ever considered that they are living in a sexless marriage? Obviously they have no choice in the matter, or do they? "Clearly they would have to broaden their definition of sex" according to research. Some experts would suggest "oral sex, mutual masturbation, touching, fondling, cuddling, kissing, creative

fantasies---intimately connecting to each other with love fits."
Please note: The previous sentence above is not the author's, nor publisher's point of view, but given only as information to a thought provoking suggestion. However, God always has the better plan and if you seek him diligently; "He" will guide you in any calamity. Your mishap did not catch "Him" by surprise since "He knows the beginning from the end." What the devil (terminator) meant for evil, "God" will use that and turn it around for your good! Although we are provided with wonderful doctors, therapists, counselors, clergyman, teachers, specialists, books, articles, etc. in their specialized fields, God knows the answer better than any man does. Ask God! *Thank you servicemen and servicewomen for your service and sacrifice and all that you do*!!!

Every relationship will have a unique dimension. Forget the blame game and be willing to take responsibility and ownership of root issues of your marital problems. Could you possibly find the courage to be respectful of each other's feelings and nonjudgmental? Negotiating and compromising is an ongoing continuously process. Don't expect everything to be solved overnight? There are no easy answers or a quick fix.

What gives someone the right to measure how often he or she should be having sex in order to be "normal"? According to

CONCLUSION

Dr. Phil "he encourages people to discuss their needs openly with their partners and negotiate a relationship that meets both of their needs."